BioBalance 2

Achieving Optimum Health
Through Acid/Alkaline Nutrition

Rudolf A. Wiley, Ph.D

© 2002 by Essential Science Publshing.
800-336-6308 • www.essentialscience.net

Printed in the United States of America
First Printing January 2002

ISBN 0-943-68533-8

DISCLAIMER: The information contained in this book is for educational purposes only. It is not provided to diagnose, prescribe, or treat any condition of the body. The information in this book should not be used as a substitute for medical counseling with a health professional. Neither the author nor publisher accepts responsibility for such use or guarantees the outcomes of following the regimens in this book.

Dedication

To my wife, Pam, and my mother, Anne, my human guardian angels

To my two beautiful daughters, Jennifer and Suzanne.

And to the memory of George Watson, PhD.
*May his monumental work in psychometabolism finally
receive the recognition it has long deserved.*

Table of Contents

Foreword iii

Prologue vii

Chapter 1 • What is BioBalance Therapy? 1

Chapter 2 • The Premier Nutritional Regimens 33

Chapter 3 • Your Personal Metaboloic Makeover 49

Chapter 4 • Myra L. — An Alkaline Metabolizer 63

Chapter 5 • Gloria R. — An Acid Metabolizer 89

Chapter 6 • Paul H. — A Mixed Mode Metabolizer 117

Chapter 7 • Kimberly B. — A Cyclic Metabolizer 139

Chapter 8 • Conclusion 149

Appendix 165

   I. Nutritional Regimen For Alkaline Metabolizers 167

   II. Nutritional Regimen for Acid Metabolizers 173

   III. Nutritional Regimen for Mixed Mode Metabolizers 181

References 191

Biography 193

Index 195

Foreword

Everything happens in the fullness of time. Some things happen in the nick of time. BioBalance is one of those things that happen in the nick of time. BioBalance is coming to the forefront as health care in the United States is entering the most severe crisis in its history. In 1960, health care costs accounted for about 6.2% of the Gross National Product (GNP). In 1990, they had accelerated to 12.9% of the GNP. By the year 2000 health care consumed about 14% of the GNP, and projections for 2010 are that it will reach 17.2%. (Source: Organization for Economic Cooperation and Development: Health Data, 1997)

It has been estimated that by the year 2050, health care costs will consume most of the GNP, if they continue to increase at their present rate. Obviously this is an intolerable situation. The government and private insurance companies already have a remedy. It is called rationing. It means that a government or insurance company clerk is likely to have a major part in deciding what health care you get and don't get. Decisions that heretofore have been made by you and your doctor may in the future be made by an employee of the government or an insurance company. This is not a cheerful picture when you consider that at least one insurance company has been reported to be paying its clerks bonuses on the basis of how many claims they deny.

Your best solution to this crisis is to get well if you aren't well, and to stay well if you are well. This solves the problem on two levels: it keeps you out of a health care system over which you will have little control and which probably won't have the resources to respond to your needs. On a more fundamental level, it saves money so that there will be more resources for those who can't help getting sick. If you like the wellness solution better than the sickness-and-rationing solution, then BioBalance comes in the nick of time because it gives you the power to push your odds far in the direction of wellness and away from sickness.

I have practiced medicine for thirty-three years and have experience with many different ways of improving health. BioBalance is the most powerful approach I have yet encountered with the possible exception of appropriate physical activity . . . and some people have to achieve BioBalance before they have even enough energy for appropriate physical activity! Combine BioBalance and physical activity and you have a physical way to wellness that is a long way ahead of whatever is second best. If BioBalance were very expensive, it would still be a bargain . . . but it isn't very expensive. In fact, once you buy the instructional materials and get some coaching if you need it, BioBalance doesn't cost you anything for the rest of your life unless you choose to use the moderately priced supplements that go with the program.

The main part of the BioBalance program uses foods available in any supermarket. You have to buy some kind of groceries anyway. Why not let BioBalance show you how to find out which foods help make you well and which make you sick? BioBalance is a uniquely powerful health enhancement system that is remarkably economical to use; in fact, it has a uniquely favorable cost-effectiveness ratio. It also has a uniquely favorable time-effectiveness ratio. In seven years of studying and practicing wellness medicine I have learned enough things that people can do to raise their level of wellness to keep anybody busy full-time just practicing a wellness program. Most people would like to have some time left over to do other things. BioBalance is for these people. Once you learn it, BioBalance only takes a negligible amount of time each day.

Before I began to use the BioBalance program for myself, I thought I had a state-of-the-art wellness program; after all, wellness is what I do for a living. I felt reasonably well. Four days after beginning BioBalance, I was feeling better than I could ever remember in my 57-year life. I had the strongest experience of well-being, the most physical and mental energy, mental clarity, creativity, and comfortableness in my body that I had ever experienced. And it has gotten better from there. Not everyone will improve that fast, but some will. Others may have to be on the appropriate foods and supplements for two or three months before experiencing maximum benefits.

But whether the progress is quick or slow, since I have been prescribing BioBalance for my patients, I have seen more patients make more progress faster toward wellness than I had seen in any other equal period of time in 33 years of medical practice.

What makes BioBalance so powerful? There is an old South Georgia saying, "If you can get hold of one kudzu root you can shake the whole state." This is because when you dig into the ground where there are kudzu roots, it looks as though each root is connected to every other root in an endless web. Henry David Thoreau once wrote, "For every person hewing to the root of the tree of evil, there are hundreds hacking at its branches." BioBalance enables you to deal with a physical root cause of health problems by improving your metabolism. Metabolism is the process by which food is changed into protoplasm, the stuff that the cells of the body are made from. It is also the process that turns food into energy. In other words, metabolism is all the chemical reactions that turn food into YOU and into the energy you must have in order to function. When you improve your metabolism you improve the overall efficiency by which your body does its biochemical business. You improve the functioning of every cell, tissue, organ, and system in your body ... and you FEEL the improvement in your mind and in your body.

This was illustrated vividly by a young woman who came in recently for a follow-up visit. I had seen her two weeks before when she was suicidally depressed. She and I were both afraid that she was going to commit suicide. We discussed hospitalization, but she was not willing to accept that. We already knew that she was an acid metabolic type.

She had been drinking beer and getting up in the middle of the night to eat fruit sugar by the tablespoonful. Either activity can make an acid metabolic type such as herself very sick and in her case it looked as though it would actually be fatal. I told her that I thought that if she could hang on, not try to kill herself, and be fanatical about following the nutritional regimen appropriate for her biochemical type, within a few days she would be feeling much better. We were both still uneasy about her condition when she left the office and I urged her to call me if she got any worse. She came back in two weeks looking like a different person. Instead of being frantic and distraught, she radiated joy, energy and self-confidence. Her skin glowed and her eyes sparkled. She talked about her utter amazement at the fact that what she ate could have such a powerful effect on the way she felt and functioned. She wanted to know how many physicians were prescribing BioBalance. As we went over her diet diaries it was clear that she began to improve after three days on the nutritional regimen appropriate for acid metabolizers. After five days, she wrote on her diary, "No negative thoughts (maybe a few)." On the following day she wrote, "No negative thoughts!"

Her progress was steady except for two occasions when she briefly went off the diet and was promptly reminded of why she was on it. It is easy to tell you that two weeks previously she had been dangerously suicidal and now she was full of life and energy. It is very hard to convey to you the glow, clarity, and joy that she radiated. I have seen this in other patients who have brought themselves into BioBalance. I have not seen it so soon or with such intensity with any other kind of treatment.

One of the greatest joys and highest fulfillments of my professional life is to participate in and observe such a transformation in my patients. I would love to live in a world where EVERYONE enjoyed this level of wellness. I believe that this is the birthright of every human being. BioBalance can be an important key to taking possession of that birthright!

Rudolf Wiley has spent 20 years developing BioBalance. His work should win a Nobel Prize because it is a way to do ONE THING that improves EVERYTHING about the way you feel and function physically and mentally . . . costs very little . . . and takes practically no time. BioBalance also offers you a way to be part of the solution to the present health care crisis rather than part of the problem.

Here it is, in the nick of time... why not GO FOR IT!

O. Jack Woodard, MD, Director
The Southeast Wellness Center, Albany, Georgia

Prologue

This book, the sequel to my first book, **BIOBALANCE: The Acid/Alkaline Solution to the Food-Mood-Health Puzzle**, is the culmination of a 30-year effort involving thousands of individuals and volumes of research data. The names and characters in each case history are fictitious. Any resemblance to actual persons either living or deceased is purely coincidental. For the sake of brevity and for illustrative purposes, some case histories are composite sketches drawn from several studies. This book makes available to the public fundamental information that has the potential to completely change the way we view and treat mental and physical disorders.

Early in my career as a physicist I was fascinated by what is known as the Mind/Body Problem - quantifying or describing in scientific terms and according to the laws of physics, the link between the mind and the body. After studying physics to the master's level, I completed a doctoral program in psychology to fully understand the connection between the physical world and the intriguing world of "the mind." However, my approach to the study of psychology was that of the trained scientist, i.e., to look for inconsistencies in methodology in order to discover why they existed and how they could be remedied. Much to my chagrin I found that there were numerous approaches to the study and treatment of mental disorders but none of them were really consistent in their data. None could be statistically validated according to the methods I had been trained in during my study of physics. I found that none of the dozens of "labels" given mental disorders could satisfactorily describe the underlying mechanisms which create the disorders.

I then did what any good scientist would do: I looked for a new set of variables. Because I had, by happy accident, stumbled upon the work of

Dr. George Watson in the field of glucose oxidation and its effect on the psychological states of individuals, I chose to look at acid/alkaline biochemistry as it pertained to mental disorders. The results of my review of hundreds of patient records where venous plasma pH, a measure of the blood's relative acidity and alkalinity, was routinely done, revealed a strong correlation: one that deserved the attention of anyone truly committed to alleviating the suffering I observed while studying and gathering data in a state mental hospital. I was excited by my findings, and being a young and enthusiastic idealist I was certain that as soon as I presented my data to "the powers that be" both in the university and in the hospital administration, work in acid/alkaline biochemistry would commence and soon the doors of the hospital would fly open, as patients recovered and issued forth in a great flood.

At the very least I felt certain that I would be asked to conduct extensive research in the area of nutrition and its effect on mental disorders as the first step in opening those doors. My suggestion to the administration, "Let's divide the patient population in half, you continue to treat your half by conventional methods - drugs, electroshock, and "the talking cure," and I'll do nothing more for my half than change their diets!"

Sadly, my data and suggestions were poorly received by both the hospital and the university. I so shook up the establishment with my outrageous idea that there was a strong link between food and mood that they chewed me up and spit me out, almost literally, not with the Ph.D. for which I had written my dissertation on the mind/body connection, but with a master's degree and a kick-in-the-pants-here's-your-hat-what's-your-hurry kind of exit. Those in psychology who had spent half their lives studying "relationships," simply refused to consider the relationship between what we eat and what we feel.

After this debacle I spent the following few years working on another Ph.D. in biological physics continuing to try to mathematically articulate the relationship between biochemistry and psycho physiological function. I received my Ph.D. not uneventfully. There was real confusion over whether my work should be judged by someone from the medical school, the department of mathematics, the biology department or the department of physics. Eventually this awkward problem was resolved and my Ph.D. was granted. However, I was no longer quite the idealist I had been. I seriously considered medical school at this point and in fact applied to several, but I also had three strikes against me: Strike one - I was too old to be considered seriously by most medical schools. Strike two - I had already spent several years bucking the establishment in psychology and physics. Medical school could only be worse. And the third strike was the climate in this country regarding health care at the time. Anyone exercising, taking vitamins, and eating "healthful" foods *on purpose* was considered to be a "health nut," an expression you rarely hear today, but in the mid seventies was still prevalent. People were not yet ready or informed enough to begin taking responsibility for their own health and well being. Physicians and psychiatrists were still the high priests of our society, and anyone outside of mainstream medical care, attempting to make waves was sure to get drowned.

Having come to this painful realization. I continued to gather and review data, and worked gratis with friends, acquaintances and referrals from those whom I had helped. Over the years the number of those helped continued to grow and this theory of acid/alkaline nutrition became more than just opinion. In the '80s, great cultural emphasis was placed on physical fitness, appearance and diet. Doctors began writing books on diets which they claimed could alleviate or cure various problems such as high cholesterol and heart disease, hyperactivity in children, premenstrual syndrome, and even stress and anxiety, two purely "mental" states now linked to food! How the world changed in 20 or so years! Now dawned the age of the "holistic M.D." and "alternative health care practitioners." The phenomenal success of books on exercise and diet, and the box office business being done by the holistic physician indicated to me that the time to introduce BioBalance Therapy had finally come, and in 1989 my first book introducing BioBalance therapy was published. The response from many of those who read that book, and their success in finally achieving a state of mental and physical health (which had been denied them for years through traditional methods of health care) was truly gratifying.

However this is not an overnight success story. Being a non-M.D. offering a health care service I was dogged again by the establishment. No matter how dramatic and long-awaited the improvement in health experienced by my clients, the bottom line for a public long accustomed to being reimbursed by their insurance companies for any and all health related services—even though they were frequently abysmal failures—

was frequently, "Will I get reimbursed?" My clients often met with strong resistance from their health insurance companies. My work was not to receive the sanction of the multi-billion dollar medical insurance industry. And most individuals found it very difficult, perhaps understandably so, to make even a modest financial commitment to this relatively unknown, albeit highly successful approach to total health care.

So I now present my work to you, dear reader, in terms that are simple, and more straightforward than ever before, so you can experience for yourself the miracle of BioBalance Therapy. It is my fondest hope that this book will break down the financial and political barriers that have prevented me from sharing BioBalance Therapy in the past.

We now live in a country where 60% to 80% of all patients seen by physicians suffer diffuse and undiagnosable symptoms. Some undergo extensive, invasive testing. Some are given various drugs to reduce symptoms. Some physicians have become lazy. They read the lab test printouts, see the statement "within normal limits," believe it, and refer their patients for counseling or psychiatric "help."

Traditional medicine, a multi-billion dollar industry, is failing as many as 3 out of 4 people in this country. This is truly a crime, and often a crime of omission when you discover how many worthwhile, valuable theories and realities, such as BioBalance Therapy, are being ignored or viciously attacked by an establishment mentality that is desperately determined to guard its territory. Medicine and psychiatry have shared the throne as "kings of the mountain" in this country and too often are closed to new paradigms and approaches that can explain and solve present health care mysteries.

I am asking that you judge the accuracy and efficacy of this book and BioBalance Therapy, not on the basis of my credentials, or lack of them, but on the body of data which I present in as interesting and understandable a fashion as I can. I know that if you do this you will conclude that what you are about to read is simply and profoundly the truth.

Dr. Rudolf Wiley
December 2001

Chapter
1

What is BioBalance Therapy?

You have just survived a catastrophic car crash. You are losing blood rapidly. As you are being rushed into the operating room you overhear a surgical nurse ask your emergency room physician what blood type will be required for your transfusion. You are horrified to hear your physician respond by stating that blood type is unimportant. He instructs his nurse to select blood at random and begin your transfusion immediately.

Such a situation is, of course, unthinkable in the practice of modern medicine. Yet in another medical context it happens thousands of times daily. With very few exceptions, virtually all physicians fail to recognize the fact that *one key or critical aspect of your personal biochemistry* dictates the foods you must eat if you are to avoid chronic, incapacitating illness, and thereby optimize your physical and mental well being. (I refer to your personal biochemistry as *your BioProfile*, a subject I will shortly discuss in more detail).

Each of us has a unique biochemical makeup. If you eat in a fashion that is not compatible with your personal biochemistry, then you will very likely suffer any one of a number of significant—if not incapacitating—disorders, which will be misdiagnosed by the health care community. If you have been unsuccessful in getting assistance from orthodox or mainstream physicians for these disorders, then you have likely been told that everything is "within normal limits." Your physicians have also probably misdiagnosed your disorders as psychological, psychogenic, mental, behavioral, attitudinal, stress-related, or stress-induced. You have probably also been shuffled off to a psychiatrist, clinical psychologist, mental health counselor, or (more recently) a stress management expert.

If on the other hand, you have been seeking assistance from a holistic physician, an alternative/complementary health care practitioner, or a nutritionist, then your problems may have been linked to other less important aspects of your biochemistry. The root cause of your disorder has in turn been incorrectly identified as any one of a combination of the following: food allergies and sensitivities, candidiasis (systemic yeast infection), weak adrenals, Epstein-Barr syndrome, hypoglycemia, pancreatitis, hypomagnesia, chronic fatigue syndrome, hypothyroidism, fibromyalgia, suppressed immune system activity, systemic mercury poisoning caused by the amalgam fillings in your teeth, etc., and this list goes on and on and on.

Tragically, most mainstream physicians are unaware of the fact that a compatible match between your nutritional regimen and your BioProfile is the single most important determinant of your physical and mental health. So they completely disregard nutrition in treating you. On the other hand, while holistic physicians, alternative/complementary health care practitioners, and nutritionists do feel that nutrition is important, almost all of these health care providers don't know anything about your BioProfile, let alone how to determine it, or how to bio-compatibly match one or more nutritional regimens with your BioProfile. These well-intentioned practitioners may configure your diet based upon factors which they feel are critically important, but which I will soon demonstrate are at best only peripherally related to your condition.

I've already listed some of the factors that health care providers claim are the root cause of your distress. For all their good intentions, these practitioners are, in the final analysis, really assigning you a diet at random. If by chance that diet is somewhat compatible with your BioProfile, then you will experience some relief. Conversely, if that diet is incompatible with your BioProfile then you will remain ill, or worse still you will mentally and physically deteriorate. Sadly some practitioners may interpret your downward spiral into disease as part of a *discharge reaction* ("you'll have to get worse before you get better") - and therefore as a good sign. Worse still, your failure to respond favorably may be interpreted as a sign of a "deep seated mental or emotional problem." You'll soon see why both of these interpretations couldn't be further from the truth.

In my first book, **BIOBALANCE: Using Acid/Alkaline Nutrition to Solve the Food-Mood-Health Puzzle**, I showed that without exception, every person possesses a BioProfile that can be rigorously and accurately classified in terms of *a key biochemical component called a metabolic index or marker.* It will come as no surprise to you that this key metabolic index or marker is defined in terms of *relative shifts in a specific component of your blood's acid/alkaline biochemistry.* I'll have more to say about this topic soon.

Appropriately matching a nutritional regimen with your BioProfile is easy to understand. If you are given a transfusion with blood, which is compatible with your blood type, then your chances of recovery increase. If you are given a transfusion with blood, which is incompatible with your blood type, then you will almost certainly die. Similarly, if you are assigned a nutritional regimen that is compatible with your BioProfile, then you will likely thrive. If on the other hand, you are assigned a nutritional regimen that is completely incompatible with your BioProfile, then you will become so ill, both mentally and physically, that you risk becoming completely nonfunctional within a few days if not within a few hours. No, I'm not exaggerating when I state that *complete bio-incompatibility*—a total mismatch between your BioProfile and your assigned nutritional regimen— is *that destructive*. I'll even show you how you can test this statement if you are foolish enough to try it.

Notice once again that I used the words *compatible* and *incompatible*, or *bio-compatible* and *bio-incompatible*, respectively. I did not use the following words, "wholesome," "nutritious," "sensible," "common sense," "reasonable," "natural," "wonderful," "healthful," "healthy" or "well-balanced." This second group of words has little meaning in the vocabulary of BioBalance Therapy, the approach to total health that you will find herein. Now, even though I have not yet discussed the *one key metabolic index* or *marker* which defines your BioProfile—which I will do shortly in layperson's language—you are prepared to understand the following fundamental definition of the term *BioBalance Therapy*.

BioBalance Therapy is a nutritional application of rigorously derived and scientifically tested principles. This application allows your physical and mental wellness to peak or optimize as follows:

- BioBalance Therapy first determines your BioProfile. This may be done non-invasively (without the use of blood tests), and without lengthy questionnaires. *In fact, a true/false response to a single simple question adequately determines one's BioProfile in the overwhelming majority of cases.*
- Depending upon your BioProfile, BioBalance Therapy assigns to you a biocompatible nutritional regimen, and companion set of biocompatible vitamin/mineral supplements.

While some nutritional regimens recommended by BioBalance Therapy will seem to obey the laws of "common sense" as defined by the so-called medical and nutritional experts, others will not. The nutritional regimens I'll be describing in this book have been developed through exhaustive and rigorous scientific investigation

Achieving peak wellness in the safest possible fashion is in many ways similar to climbing a mountain. You should think of this book as a written guide to climbing a mountain. In this context, the information in the book details the safest and easiest route you must take to reach the mountain's summit or peak. Reaching the mountain's peak should therefore be viewed as your primary *objective*. Finding the safest and easiest route to that peak would therefore be viewed as the *approach* I've planned for you in achieving this objective. Analogously, your objective in reading this book should consist of understanding the critical importance of eating biocompatibly as defined within the context of BioBalance Therapy. In other words, your objective should consist of understanding that if you eat biocompatibly, you will achieve peak psychological and physical wellness. Conversely, you should also understand that by eating in a bio-incompatible fashion, you run the risk of becoming ill within a very short period of time. Consequently, your objectives in reading this book — like reading my first book — should be similar if not formally identical: reaching peak wellness. On the other hand, the approach (or the path allowing you to achieve that objective) which I outline in this book, differs substantially from the approach used in my first book, most notable in the sense that <u>no blood tests are required</u>.

Specifically, in the 2-step approach I outline in this book:

- I will show you how to determine your BioProfile without the use of blood tests, and without the use of lengthy questionnaires. In this regard, *I'll show you how a simple yes/no answer to only one key question can, in the overwhelming majority of cases, reveal your BioProfile.*
- I will also show you how to apply a reformulated version of each of the original biocompatible nutritional regimens I originally created almost 30 years ago. Each of these original biocompatible nutritional regimens was (*and still is*) appropriate for each of the respective static metabolic types. As you will see, this book contains new and updated versions of the original regimens. By using these reformulated regimens, BioBalance Therapy's success rate (previously observed to be 90%+) is further enhanced.

So, while the objective is still the same, *the two major simplifications made in this book help make BioBalance Therapy more 1) fool-proof and 2) fail-proof,* respectively. This is accomplished in a direct how-to/hands-on manner which almost anyone can understand, without engaging in a detailed discussion of the emotionally and politically charged issues which are part of the controversy surrounding mainstream and holistic health care, nutrition and psychotherapy.

Among other reasons, I wrote this book in response to numerous inquiries I received regarding my first book in which I discussed a remarkable discovery made while a psychology graduate student almost 30 years ago. That discovery was the extremely strong correlation between a *biochemical marker* called *venous plasma pH* and how you feel emotionally, mentally and physically.

I hasten once again to add that you need not understand "venous plasma pH" to understand the information I provide in this book. So, if you are not scientifically oriented, *continue reading anyway*. It is written for the layperson who has no in-depth knowledge of organic chemistry, metabolic activity or mathematics. Nonetheless, research references are provided at the end of the book for readers who desire information of a technical nature. Venous plasma pH, which may be reliably and predictably controlled by nutritional means, is an integral part of BioBalance Therapy's scientific foundation. Venous plasma pH is the measure of *relative* acidity and *relative* alkalinity of blood flowing through your veins. (If you have ever gardened or owned a swimming pool, you already know that pH is a measure of your soil's or water's acid/alkaline balance respectively. In this regard, pH is a common acid/alkaline indicator that is not at all unique to BioBalance Therapy.)

In the context of BioBalance Therapy however, the measure of your blood's relative acid/alkaline balance is extremely important, since it indicates how efficiently the cells in your entire body convert the food you eat (literally, the fuel you consume) into the energy which you use for *all* activities extending from hard physical exercise to thinking, sleeping, dreaming, as well as *emoting* or feeling. You may think that the word *emoting* is peculiar, but I use it here to describe how you emotionally respond to the unavoidable stresses and strains of life. In other words, do you psychologically respond to difficult situations adaptively and resiliently, or does the slightest stress psychologically shatter you, or make you act impulsively in a manner you may later regret? It is important to understand that achieving a state of BioBalance will not make you mono-emotional (emotionally flat), and immune to life. In this regard, BioBalance Therapy will not protect you from life. To paraphrase Shakespeare, you will still be the target of life's "slings and arrows of outrageous fortune." BioBalance Therapy will simply shape the manner in which you respond.

You will also note that I used the word *relative* in referring to your blood pH because *all human blood is always alkaline with respect to distilled water whose pH is neutral.* Consequently, the shifts in venous plasma pH values to which I refer are relative shifts on the alkaline side of the pure distilled water spectrum. Because so many of my first book's readers wanted to know how they could instantaneously and repeatedly measure their venous plasma pH to determine and (unnecessarily) reassess their nutritional regimens, I set about to find an alternative method which could enable you to instantaneously, painlessly and accurately determine your BioProfile free of charge. I touched upon this method in the "How-To" section of my first book.

Since my first book was published, I have helped numerous physicians determine their BioProfiles and their patients' BioProfiles through interviews and trial-and-error techniques. Since then, I have found a simpler diagnostic technique, and will make this new and improved technique (which in the overwhelming majority of cases, involves only a single criterion) available to you. I would however urge you to read my first book if you would like to understand in detail how BioBalance Therapy works, and how it can help both primary and alternative health care better solve the problems connected with poor psychological or emotional health as well as poor physical health.

BioBalance is a real, replicable and physically *quantifiable* biochemical state that is achieved when venous plasma pH is neither too low (too acid - *relatively* speaking) nor too high (too alkaline - *relatively* speaking) as measured about a set point. Once again, the relative acid/alkaline shifts to which I refer are measured around a set point that is *not* neutral, but which is alkaline with respect to pure distilled water. Very small variations from this set point can have a profound affect on a person's physical *and* mental well-being

Because it is based on scientific, measurable principles, BioBalance is not some vague, nebulous, mystical and poetic metaphor for feeling well. Biologically, the state of BioBalance is quantifiable and real. As your venous plasma pH changes by as little as 1%, you may experience subtle changes in your feelings of personal well being. When your venous plasma pH changes by 2%, the accompanying changes in your sense of well being will be clearly evident to you. When your venous plasma pH changes by 3% or more, try as you may, you will not be able to hide positive or negative behavioral changes.

Herein lies the formidable power of BioBalance Therapy. As the references listed at the end of this book show, these changes cannot be ascribed to the *placebo effect* or *power of suggestion*. They can be objectively monitored independently through any one of a number of well-established and objective tests called *multiphasic inventories*. You need not be familiar with these inventories either, in order to understand the information in this book. Suffice it to say that the results achieved through BioBalance Therapy are measurable, replicable, physiological responses.

If you are a health care professional you may balk when I discuss changes in venous plasma pH because you have been trained to believe that venous plasma pH does not change by very much. You are correct in believing this. However, and as I've already stated, the changes I'm discussing are significant to 1 part in 100. Incidentally, state-of-the-art, off-the-shelf, commercially available pH meters can rapidly and inexpensively measure these changes. But once again, it is my intent to show you how you may by-pass these tests, and *instantaneously* and *accurately* determine your BioProfile and that of your patients *at no cost.*

Human venous plasma pH is in some respects like the pH of water in a swimming pool or soil in a flower or vegetable garden. In a swimming pool or garden, bacteria and fungus will thrive if pool water or soil is not pH balanced, thus creating numerous problems for the pool's owner or gardener. As any experienced gardener knows, buying the most "wonderful," "natural," "sensible," "nutritious," "wholesome," "healthy," or "reasonable," plant food and fertilizer is a waste of time and money if your soil's pH is not first appropriately adjusted through the application of specialized nutrients.

Similarly, an overly acid or overly alkaline metabolic condition (as measured by venous plasma pH) increases the probability that you will suffer from a wide variety of symptoms and problems which are routinely misdiagnosed by both the medical and alternative health care communities. These conditions may be characterized by chronic fatigue, insomnia, depression, situation-specific or free-floating anxiety, panic disorders, obsessive-compulsive disorders (OCDs), poor ability to focus attention, undiagnosable body aches and headaches, gastrointestinal and absorption/elimination problems such as "nervous stomach," "irritable bowel," menstrual syndrome problems, including premenstrual syndrome (PMS), or more recently premenstrual dystrophic disorder (PMDD), countless weight related/weight management problems, etc., and this list goes on and on. Incidentally, these conditions make up more than 50% of all complaints heard by primary health care practitioners on a daily basis.

I've already mentioned that these disorders are commonly and erroneously misdiagnosed as mental, psychological, psychogenic, psychiatric, behavioral, attitudinal, and stress-related. I can state unequivocally that these disorders have little if anything in common with such labels. The genesis or root of these disorders has also more recently been ascribed to such conditions as candidiasis (systemic yeast infections), Epstein-Barr Syndrome, hypoglycemia, hypomagnesia, pancreatitis, weak adrenals, food allergies, suppressed immune system activity, leaky gut syndrome, etc., and this list also goes on and on. While these diagnoses (unlike those which are psychologically oriented) have some merit in limited applications, they also do not accurately describe the fundamental underlying cause of your distress, which is almost always a relative acid/alkaline imbalance in blood biochemistry. This in turn reflects an inefficient conversion of fuel (food) to energy at the cellular level throughout your entire body. Incidentally, this fuel-to-energy conversion inefficiency is the definition of a *biochemical* or *metabolic imbalance* or *dysfunction*.

Just as each person has his or her own unique set point for venous plasma pH, so each person has his or her own unique metabolic pattern. There are three primary, *static* metabolic types or states. I use the word *static* to denote unchanging over time. (A significant minority of individuals (primarily women) possess metabolic states which change or *cycle* in time. I'll discuss these *cyclic types* or *cyclic BioProfiles* later.)

I classify these three primary metabolic types or states as acid, alkaline and mixed mode. We determine a person's metabolic type by his or her mental and physical responses to the foods he or she eats as follows.

When randomly eating a broad variety of foods:

- acid metabolizers will become excessively and relatively acidic (venous plasma pH will decrease), and will suffer a subsequent erosion of physical and mental health.
- alkaline metabolizers will become excessively and relatively alkalotic (venous plasma pH will increase), and will suffer a subsequent erosion of physical and mental health.
- mixed metabolizers will become excessively and relatively acidic (but not as acidic as acid metabolizers), and will suffer a subsequent erosion of physical and mental health.

Humans are *metabolically diverse* because of *genetic factors*. (I briefly mentioned the genetic basis of *metabolic diversity* in my first book, but a discussion of genetics lies far beyond the scope of this book.) Note, as I will show later, random ingestion of food will not necessarily result in a nutritional mismatch. Therefore erosion of health resulting from random ingestion of food can either be severe or mild, and can occur over very short periods of time (hours), or longer periods of time (months or years) respectively.

As stated previously, intentionally consuming foods to achieve a complete nutritional mismatch within the context of BioBalance Therapy will accelerate and compress this erosion process to a matter of days or even hours! Having watched this happen on numerous occasions, I am not exaggerating when I make this claim. The critical point here is that each metabolic type must eat in a way that will counter effect, offset or neutralize his or her respective underlying metabolic tendency if he or she wishes to achieve and maintain a state of BioBalance leading to optimal physical and mental wellness.

Not surprisingly then, acid types must eat foods that are alkalinizing or alkaline-inducing. Alkaline types must eat foods that are acidifying or acid-inducing. Mixed types must eat foods that are alkalinizing, but not as alkalinizing as those foods appropriate for acid types. This book will show you exactly how to do this.

These fundamental laws of BioBalance are based upon *both deductive* and *inductive* scientific processes. The former means that the laws of BioBalance can be deduced via first principles of metabolic theory (called *metabolic rate kinetics*), which have been substantiated time and time again. The latter means that the conclusions arrived at or deduced using these first principles have been confirmed by a statistically significant number of observations through double blind placebo-controlled trials (see references). This rigorous two-pronged approach in establishing BioBalance Therapy as a science distinguishes it from other dietary health care approaches which to a large extent remain unvalidated through scientific means, thus making them little more than part of an ongoing trendy sales pitch.

If the acid/alkaline categories confuse you, let me state the basis of BioBalance Therapy in a slightly different and simplified fashion:

- There are three basic static metabolic states. At any point in time every individual will occupy one and only one of these three states. Therefore, at any point in time each individual can be classified as one and only one static metabolic type. Normally, a person's metabolic state will remain the same throughout his or her lifetime.* (See below)
- There are three and only three biocompatible nutritional regimens (each with its unique companion set of vitamin/mineral supplements). Each of these three unique regimen/supplement combinations will enable its respective static metabolic type or recipient to achieve peak psychological and physical wellness. Peak wellness is achieved by counter effecting or neutralizing the underlying metabolic imbalance. Counter effecting or neutralizing an underlying imbalance is achieved when the individual in question adheres to his/her biocompatible regimen. Consequently, BioBalance Therapy does not provide a "cure," but provides instead a method of control, free of side effects, which allows the body to maximize its own performance.
- Conversely, mismatching a nutritional regimen/supplement combination with a metabolic type will erode wellness and performance, and will eventually bring about illness. The extent of the mismatch (partial to total) will in turn determine the severity of the resultant imbalance and eventual disease. It will also determine the

---

* A few individuals transition from one static metabolic state to another during the following critical physiological milestones:
- the onset of puberty (typically between the ages of 10 and 13)
- the cessation of significant physical growth (typically between the ages of 18 and 21)
- the onset of menopause (typically between the ages 40 and 60)
- during pregnancy and/or the cessation of lactation.

Incidentally, pregnancy-related and lactation-related changes in BioProfile are almost always the underlying reason for the onset of Post Partum Depression. Post Partum Depression is not the result of the many so-called psychological, mental or behavioral factors, which the psychotherapeutic community has long held sacred.

With few exceptions, cyclically repetitive changes in metabolic type are peculiar to premenopausal women. I should however emphasize that a premenopausal woman does not of necessity possess a cyclic BioProfile. The case history mentioned later in this book as well as the case histories provided in my first book amply illustrate this point.

amount of time it will take for the imbalance and companion illness to present themselves. Clearly then, when an individual has achieved a state of BioBalance and then reverts to a nutritional regimen that does not neutralize his or her metabolic imbalance (a bio-incompatible diet), then the underlying imbalance and its accompanying illnesses will recur.

BioBalance Therapy's success rate in terms of positive outcomes, consistently reaches 90% or higher. Double blind studies verify that its success has nothing to do with the placebo effect, commonly known as power of suggestion.

It is important to understand that each static metabolic type requires one and only one nutritional regimen both to *achieve* and *maintain* BioBalance. Some readers of my first book wrote to me asking if the dietary regimens I outlined only enabled each metabolic type to *achieve* BioBalance, thinking that once BioBalance was achieved, a *different* but standard regimen for all metabolic types was then required for all metabolic types to *maintain* BioBalance. These readers erroneously jumped to the conclusion that acid and alkaline metabolic activity described the extreme ends of the metabolic spectrum, so mixed metabolic activity described a state of relative BioBalance. This led to the further mistaken conclusion that the nutritional regimen recommended for a mixed metabolic type was the BioBalance "maintenance diet." (Still other readers erroneously jumped to the conclusion that yet another (fourth) diet similar to a macrobiotic diet— also discussed later in this book—was required for "maintenance" once BioBalance was achieved.) All of these conclusions are incorrect. So I will reiterate this one point to eliminate any confusion: while some fine tuning may be required in a few cases (examples are provided in this book), you will NOT need to substantially modify your biocompatible nutritional regimen as you approach BioBalance in order to compensate for the fact that your pre-existing metabolic imbalance is lessening as you make that approach. Your body automatically does that via a mechanism called an *autocompensatory response*. A detailed discussion of that mechanism lies beyond the scope of this book. In plain English, my research shows that *each metabolic state requires one and only one nutritional regimen to both **achieve** and **maintain** BioBalance.*

Let me summarize the three basic principles I've outlined above.

- If you eat in a fashion that is appropriate for or compatible with your metabolic type, your psychological and physical wellness and performance will peak.

- Conversely, if you eat in a fashion, which is inappropriate for, or incompatible with your metabolic type, you will move away from optimal wellness and will gradually or precipitously become sick. Your illness will likely present itself as a so-called psychological, mental, behavioral or stress-related problem, but it may also present itself as a readily identifiable physical or medical problem.

- Finally, if you eat in random fashion, or in a fashion *not* prescribed by BioBalance, *you will drift into and out of states of relative wellness without knowing why.* Indeed, without being familiar with BioBalance Therapy, you may unwittingly attribute the alteration in your state of relative wellness to factors that have little if anything to do with the metabolic and nutritional mechanism which is in fact responsible for your physiological and mental health.

Having described these metabolic types and the principles underlying BioBalance Therapy, what should each of these metabolic types eat in order to increase their probability of achieving BioBalance or optimal wellness? A detailed description of how each metabolic type must eat is listed in this book's appendix. A brief summary analysis is given later in this chapter; nonetheless, I would urge you to study the dietary information in the appendix carefully *before* reading further because the nutritional regimen appropriate for *your* BioProfile is listed there.

How do I know that *your* biocompatible regimen is listed in the appendix? Because *every single human being possesses a BioProfile, and it will be one of the three* static metabolic states I have explained (or, in some cases, a cyclically sequenced combination of these states). There simply are no exceptions to this rule. Consequently, no one is "immune to" or "exempt from" the implications of BioBalance Therapy. You would be mistaken (as were some of my first book's readers) if you were to conclude that BioBalance Therapy is "just for sick people, fat people and/or crazy people," and that "people who feel okay can eat whatever they want whenever they feel like it," and never pay by forfeiting good health. I'll have more to say about this later.

As I've already stated, I'll soon show you how you can determine your own BioProfile *without* the use of blood tests or lengthy questionnaires. In reading the appendix, you'll note that the nutritional regimen appropriate for alkaline metabolizers is virtually the mirror image opposite of the nutritional regimen appropriate for acid metabolizers.*

Specifically, most of the foods allowed for acid metabolizers are to be avoided by alkaline metabolizers, while most of the foods allowed for alkaline metabolizers are to be avoided by acid metabolizers. Mixed metabolizers on the other hand do best by eating a combination of these two regimens, biasing their regimen far more in favor of the regimen appropriate for acid metabolizers. Why? Because mixed metabolizers metabolically resemble acid metabolizers far more than they metabolically resemble alkaline metabolizers.

Similarly, the vitamin/mineral supplements appropriate for alkaline metabolizers are part of a subset of all the major vitamins and minerals currently available. Conversely, the vitamin/mineral supplements appropriate for acid metabolizers (also referred to as the acid-compatible supplements) are part of the mutually exclusive complementary subset of supplements appropriate for alkaline metabolizers. Why? Because acid and alkaline metabolizers are diametric opposites of each other.

It will not come as a surprise to you that the supplements appropriate for mixed metabolizers are a combination or *superposition* of these two subsets, favoring those supplements appropriate for acid metabolizers. Why? Once again, because mixed metabolizers metabolically resemble acid metabolizers far more than they metabolically resemble alkaline metabolizers.

---

* The following phrases are interchangeable:
- Appropriate for alkaline types or metabolizers = alkaline-appropriate = alkaline-compatible = acid-inducing.
- Appropriate for acid types or metabolizers = acid-appropriate = acid-compatible = alkaline-inducing.
- Appropriate for mixed types or metabolizers = mixed-appropriate = mixed-compatible = alkaline-inducing, but not as alkaline-inducing as those foods and supplements appropriate for acid metabolizers.

Note, I am not stating that each metabolic type must avoid taking certain vitamins and minerals. I am however stating that people of each metabolic type must avoid ingesting certain *supplemental* vitamins and minerals if they wish to achieve and maintain a state of BioBalance. Why? Because bio-incompatible vitamins and minerals taken in supplemental form or in addition to those ingested as part of that metabolic type's biocompatible nutritional regimen to some extent hinder that individual from achieving BioBalance.

In order to enhance your understanding of these regimens and supplements I'll give you plenty of examples in this book, and I'll give you a chance to work out a menu for your own BioProfile. Once again, I urge you to familiarize yourself with the information in the appendix *right now*, just try to get an idea of how these three nutritional regimens and companion vitamin/mineral supplements differ from each other.

Summary of the three dietary regimens

I'll now provide you with a quick-look overview of both the nutritional regimens and companion vitamin/mineral supplements compatible for each metabolic type.

The nutritional regimen appropriate for alkaline metabolizers is
(a) rich in complex carbohydrates
(b) low in fats
(c) modest in its protein content, and
(d) ideally almost completely devoid of certain proteins called *nucleoproteins* or *purines.*

What are nucleoproteins or purines? Nucleoproteins or purines, like all other proteins, consist of basic biochemical building blocks called *amino acids,* which are linked together via *biochemical bonds.* Think of these bonds as the chemical links binding the amino acid blocks together in a protein chain. The bonds in nucleoproteins however are different than the bonds that link together the amino acids in other protein chains. For the purpose of this discussion, it suffices to say that the bonds within nucleoproteins are some of the most alkaline-inducing agents naturally occurring in foods. This is precisely why the foods containing nucleoproteins or purines are to be avoided or used sparingly by alkaline metabolizers, and alkaline metabolizers only.

Conversely, for acid-metabolizers, purine-rich foods *must* form the acid metabolizer's core nutritional regimen. Purine concentration is especially high in the meats, fish and poultry allowed for acid metabolizers, far higher in fact than in purine-rich vegetables. That's why purine-rich vegetables cannot be substituted for purine-rich fish, meats and poultry in the regimens compatible for acid metabolizers and (to a lesser extent) for mixed metabolizers. In fact, I routinely tell acid metabolizers that, for them, a meal without purine-rich fish, meat or poultry is simply not a meal.

A quick look at purine-rich foods includes: dark meat fish and certain cold water fish (such as salmon, sardines, herrings, anchovies, darker meat tuna - as opposed to fancy white albacore tuna, etc.), dark meat poultry and fowl (thighs, wings and drum sticks), crustaceans, shell fish, red meats, organ meats, pork (to a lesser extent), and certain vegetables such as spinach, cauliflower, asparagus, artichokes and artichoke hearts, mushrooms, legumes (beans, peas and lentils of all varieties), nuts and seeds - especially peanuts. Almost all other foods are either relatively neutral in terms of their acid/alkaline induction capacity, or they are acid-inducing.

The neutral foods (especially whole grains) should be a critical part of *everyone's* nutritional regimen, including the regimens appropriate for acid and mixed metabolizers. Highly acid-inducing foods such as citrus, certain vegetables and certain beverages (all listed in the appendix) should be avoided by acid metabolizers and used sparingly by mixed metabolizers.

For those with concerns about eating animal products, I'll show you in Chapter Two how it's possible for acid and mixed mode metabolizers to eat lower off the food chain, avoiding red meats, organ meats, pork and poultry/fowl, without compromising their health. However, if acid metabolizers choose to eat in this fashion, they must eat allowed or biocompatible seafood. Simply stated, *vegetarianism is not a good option if you are an acid or mixed metabolizer.*

Also in Chapter Two, I'll also show you how it's possible for alkaline metabolizers to eat lower off the food chain, thereby avoiding all or most animal foods without compromising their health. Alkaline metabolizers must compensate in their diet, by avoiding alkaline-inducing foods. *In some cases, purine-deficient vegetarianism is the regimen of choice for alkaline metabolizers, and alkaline metabolizers only.*

In so far as vitamin/mineral supplements are concerned, in order to enhance the alkalinizing impact of purine-rich foods, BioBalance Therapy identifies the following core supplements as biocompatible for acid metabolizers:

Vitamin A palmitate	Vitamin E (mixed tocopherols)
Vitamin C	Niacinamide
Vitamin B12	Pantothenic Acid
Inositol	Choline
Zinc	Iodine
Calcium	Phosphorous

Conversely, the core biocompatible supplements appropriate for alkaline metabolizers are:

Vitamin A (fish liver oil)	Vitamin D
Vitamin E (d-alpha tocopherols)	Vitamin C
Vitamin B1	Vitamin B2
Vitamin B6	Niacin
Para-amino Benzoic Acid (PABA)	Folic Acid
Biotin	Potassium
Magnesium	Iron
Copper	Manganese
Chromium.	

Let me re-emphasize, I am not suggesting that any metabolic type abstain from the vitamins and minerals appropriate for its metabolic opposite. All vitamins and minerals are included in each of the three nutritional regimens defined by BioBalance Therapy. I simply suggest that it is not advisable for any metabolic type to ingest *supplemental* vitamins and minerals in any additional significant quantities if they are not biocompatible. (Each supplement's dose for each metabolic type is listed in the appendix at the end of this book.)

The idea that some people (acid-metabolizers) need a purine-rich nutritional regimen often stirs controversy within the health care community whose misguided slogan may be summed up as "Let's **ALL** eat light to live right!" I'll have more to say about the confusion, controversy, contradiction and chaos within the nutritional and health care communities later, although I suspect that after having read this much of my book, you can already see why BioBalance Therapy's concept of *metabolic diversity* readily resolves the name-calling, accusations, bickering and apparently irreconcilable contradictions within these communities. Clearly, the so-called light diets being widely promoted by the health care community today have at least three strikes against them:

- These diets are not purine-deficient enough or *light* enough to give alkaline metabolizers (the majority of the population) significant metabolic mileage. Conversely, these diets are not purine-rich or *heavy* enough (even the protein-rich "ketogenic diet" now being promoted by Dr. Richard Atkins) to give non-alkaline metabolizers (the minority of the population) any significant metabolic mileage.
- These diets do not differentiate between foods containing proteins and nucleoproteins or purines, so random selection of a diet and its subsequent application is figuratively akin to playing a game of metabolic Russian roulette.
- Popularly promoted diets are never accompanied by an appropriate set of biocompatible vitamin/mineral supplements, so the unfortunate individual who selects both an incompatible diet and an incompatible vitamin/mineral regimen may self-inflict serious metabolic damage within a very short period of time. If you are the unfortunate individual who has unwittingly selected both a bio-incompatible food regimen and a bio-incompatible vitamin/mineral regimen, the results (as I am sure you can testify) have been rapid and catastrophic. That adverse reaction alone, experienced no doubt by hundreds of thousands of individuals desperately seeking assistance from failed and hit-and-miss medical and alternative therapies, should indirectly provide ample testimony to BioBalance Therapy's dark side, namely its formidable power to inflict metabolic destruction if applied incorrectly. Fortunately, that destruction is reversible via the proper application of BioBalance Therapy, if it has not been continuously inflicted over prolonged periods of time.

Seldom do the health care providers I've spoken to over the past 30 years exhibit any knowledge or familiarity with nucleoproteins or purines, let alone the concept of biocompatibility and biochemical diversity. The few who do feel that the chemical bonds linking the amino acids together in the purine chain serve no metabolic purpose other than to link amino acids together. This misinformation enables a situation to arise where it is possible (indeed likely) that a health care practitioner will unwittingly allow an alkaline patient to eat purine-rich foods as part of a "light diet" since some purine-rich foods seem "wholesome," "sensible," "reasonable," "nutritious," "healthful," "healthy" and "good-for-you," especially if these foods are "all-natural" (whatever that means).

I hope you are beginning to see the profound implications of human biochemical diversity. Once it is understood that people have differing BioProfiles, the above descriptions are almost meaningless. An inordinately high intake of purine-rich foods can and will spell disaster if you are an alkaline metabolizer, and an inordinately low intake of purine-rich foods will do little if anything to abort an acid episode if you are a mixed mode or an acid metabolizer.

Incidentally, eating high protein fare will do *absolutely nothing* for an acid metabolizer if that fare is purine-poor. Specifically, eggs, dairy (low fat or otherwise), light meat fowl/poultry, light meat fish (all high-protein but low-purine foods) are simply not a substitute for high-purine fare, especially purine-rich seafood, meats and poultry. Trying to abort an acid episode using low-purine fare is figuratively akin to stopping a speeding freight train with a tissue paper barricade. If nutritionists and holistically-oriented health care providers spent more time studying organic chemistry, mathematics, and enzyme rate kinetics they'd understand why this is the case.

Some individuals who read my first book became confused by the fact that the acid/alkaline categories I used to classify various foods were, to some extent, at odds with pre-existing categories with which they were familiar. If you look at the appendix in this book you will see lists of foods appropriate for each metabolic type. Many individuals became confused when their attempts to compare my categories with other categories based upon different foods' ash contents ended in failure. For example, ash content suggests that red meat is acidifying. Instead, I have discovered that red meat is one of the most alkalinizing foods available (it drives venous plasma pH up). This is just one of many seeming discrepancies.

While I addressed this issue in a slightly different context in my first book, let me put it to rest now once and for all. The ash content of a food has very little to do with that food's impact upon venous plasma pH. Once again, venous plasma pH is an excellent metabolic indicator of your over-all wellness. (To be precise, when I speak about metabolism, I refer to *intermediary metabolism* and *not basal metabolism*. The former is an excellent indicator of your body's fuel-to-energy conversion efficiency. The latter is not.) A food's chemical composition is a determinant of whether that food will drive your venous plasma pH up (and will therefore be alkalinizing), or drive venous plasma pH down (and will therefore be acidifying). The acid/alkaline food categories I've listed in this book's appendix are based on hard data I've compiled (see references) which are in turn in accord with foundation principles of metabolism and biochemistry, called *metabolic rate kinetics*. This type of evidence is very difficult to refute. I can't say the same for the ash content categorization or countless other categorizations now being sold to the public. I am not aware of any underlying analysis to support an "ash-wellness connection," but I do know that if you try and apply ash based acid/alkaline categories as part of a therapeutic modality, it will backfire and may cause some serious metabolic damage. This will not happen with BioBalance Therapy if correctly applied.

A Simple Technique For Detecting BioProfile

Although the following topic is discussed in more detail in Chapter Three, I will now briefly outline how you may determine your BioProfile without the use of blood tests or lengthy questionnaires.

In a field as complex as human biochemistry there are always bound to be exceptions to the rule. Nevertheless I have found that there is an exceptionally strong correlation between the metabolic state you occupy at any time, and your response to specific foods, and one particular food or more precisely, one stimulant. That stimulant is *caffeine.*

Specifically, I have observed the following to be true in more than 99% of the cases I have counseled:

- Alkaline metabolizers have favorable reactions to caffeine. In other words, alkaline metabolizers are caffeine-tolerant. A cup of coffee (*not* the decaffeinated variety) picks them up, clears their minds, energizes them, and is generally the proverbial "cup of ambition."
- Acid metabolizers have unfavorable reactions to caffeine. In other words, acid metabolizers are caffeine-intolerant. A cup of (*non*-decaffeinated) coffee makes them extremely irritable, jumpy, jittery and nervous. It is not uncommon to hear an acid metabolizer exclaim "even one cup of coffee makes me feel as though I'm going to jump or claw my way out of my skin."
- Mixed mode metabolizers may respond favorably or neutrally to a fraction of a cup of coffee, but they generally cannot drink any more than that quantity without becoming irritable, jumpy, jittery and nervous.
- Individuals whose BioProfile is cyclic will report that their response to caffeine will differ depending upon time of the month (typically some premenopausal women) or even time of day or year.

Statistically, the frequency of occurrence of the different metabolic types in the population at large, is as follows:
- Approximately 75% of all males as well as females who do not have menstrual cycles are static alkaline.
- Fewer than 12.5% of all males as well as females who do not have menstrual cycles are static acid.
- Fewer than 12.5% of all males as well as females who do not have menstrual cycles are static mixed mode.
- Fewer than 1% of all males as well as females who do not have menstrual cycles have cyclic BioProfiles.
- Approximately 60% of all females who have menstrual cycles are static alkaline.
- Approximately 15% of all females who have menstrual cycles are static acid.
- Approximately 15% of all females who have menstrual cycles are static mixed mode.
- Approximately 10% of all females who have menstrual cycles have cyclic BioProfiles, and the overwhelming majority of these cyclic cases coincide with their menstrual cycle (circa 28 days).

If you are a premenopausal female (you have menstrual cycles) suffering from symptoms which vary cyclically with your menstrual cycle, do not automatically conclude that you possess a cyclic BioProfile unless your caffeine tolerance changes dramatically and abruptly during your menstrual cycle. If your caffeine tolerance does not change, but your symptom severity does, then this merely suggests that the static metabolic state you occupy reflects a deepening metabolic imbalance during one phase of your menstrual cycle as opposed to another.

For example, you may be alkaline throughout your entire menstrual cycle, but increasingly alkaline during your premenstrual phase. Or conversely, you may be acid throughout your menstrual cycle, but increasingly acid during your premenstrual phase.

If you routinely drink a great deal of coffee (not something I recommend for even the most alkaline metabolic type), then you have likely become caffeine-insensitive. To determine your reaction to caffeine, I would suggest that you stop drinking coffee for at least a week, and then re-introduce one cup to determine your reaction. If you do not drink coffee for religious reasons, then I would suggest that you seek a temporary medical dispensation if at all possible, or take a modified form of the food challenge test I describe later in this book. Caffeine may be excluded from that food challenge test without significantly compromising its validity.

Finally, I must emphasize that *individuals* possess BioProfiles. With one definite exception, and one likely exception, namely hypoglycemia and diabetes, respectively (which I discuss in Chapter Eight), *disorders do not possess BioProfiles.* Consequently, *there is no apparent correlation between the overwhelming majority of disorders and type of metabolic imbalance.* In other words, there are as many individuals (in pro rata share per the percentages listed earlier) suffering from chronic fatigue syndrome who are alkaline as there are individuals who are non-alkaline or cyclic. Similar statements can be made for anxiety, depression, premenstrual syndrome, fibromyalgia, etc..

Consequently, in getting to the root of your disorder, it is imperative that you first decipher your BioProfile, and not focus upon the symptoms that you display. Unfortunately, in its noble but terribly limited attempt to provide alternative treatment for disease, holistic health care has also disproportionately focused upon symptoms, and this has led to a great deal of confusion, especially in its treatment of hypoglycemia. As I discuss in greater detail in Chapter Eight (and in my first book as well), hypoglycemia is a very real disorder, which has by and large been misunderstood, misdiagnosed and improperly treated by the holistic health care community. If you or anyone you know has ever been classified as hypoglycemic, then the sections of both my books dealing with this condition are well worth reading.

The remainder of this book consists of seven additional chapters and an appendix.

- As I've already stated, this book's appendix contains detailed lists of recommended foods and foods to avoid for each static metabolic type.
- Chapter Two shows you a relatively recent discovery I made. It features three 'new-and-improved' nutritional regimens, one for each of the metabolic types. Each reformulated regimen allows the respective metabolic type to eat far lower off the food chain (focusing on plant foods rather than animal foods) without compromising the effectiveness of BioBalance Therapy. I'll explain how each of these three premier reformulated regimens enhances the effectiveness of the standard three biocompatible regimens I first formulated almost 30 years ago (listed in my first book). Specifically, one of these premier regimens allows alkaline metabolizers to engage either in a specific form of vegetarianism (if they so desire), or in quasi-vegetarianism which includes occasional ingestion of certain varieties of light meat or low-purine fish. Each of the other two premier regimens allows acid and mixed mode metabolizers respectively (each a non-alkaline class of metabolizer) to restrict their dietary intakes to certain varieties of fish and seafood only (the high purine variety), thereby allowing all non-alkaline metabolizers to avoid red meats, organ meats, pork and poultry.
- Chapter Three was written to reintroduce you to yourself, by showing you how to configure your personal metabolic makeover. Specifically, Chapter Three shows you how to determine your BioProfile *without* the use of blood tests and lengthy questionnaires, and how to track your reactions to one or more of the regimens I list so you may achieve optimal wellness.

- Chapters Four, Five and Six serve to introduce you to the case histories of three individuals possessing each of the three static BioProfiles. These individuals are alkaline, acid and mixed mode metabolizers respectively. Each of these chapters contains sample food/mood diaries.

- Chapter Seven introduces you to an individual whose BioProfile is cyclic, that is, it regularly transitions from one static metabolic state to another over time. This is more common among (but is neither peculiar to, or universally characteristic of) women who have menstrual cycles. Incidentally, cyclic variations in symptom severity (not necessarily indicative of a cyclic BioProfile) may result either from transitions between two or more metabolic states, or from hormonally magnified accentuations of one given metabolic imbalance. This is precisely why women on average are metabolically and symptomatically far more complex than men, and why women comprise more than 70% of the population seeking assistance through primary health care. Tragically, their symptoms are commonly written off as psychological, or (even worse) as neurotic or hypochondriacal in origin. Chapter 7 also contains sample food-mood diaries.

- Chapter Eight summarizes why there is so much confusion and conflict in the fields of psychotherapy, mainstream and alternative medical care, and nutrition, and how *BioBalance readily deconflicts this confusion through its revolutionary discovery of **intermediary metabolic diversity** within the human species. It also contaons additional commentary on the problems of hypoglycemia and diabetes.*

By way of summary, the matrix on page 25 provides an overview of the implications of BioBalance Therapy. Specifically, the matrix pairs off each of the three metabolically-compatible nutritional regimens (read down the extreme left hand column: Acid-Compatible, Mixed-Compatible, Alkaline-Compatible) with each of the three possible static metabolic states any individual can occupy at any point in time (read across the top row headings: Acid, Mixed, Alkaline). Consequently, there are nine possible resultant pairings, each of which is represented by one of the nine matrix entries. Each matrix entry in turn provides a synopsis of one of four possible outcomes.

BioBalance Matrix

Outcome of all possible pairings between the three metabolically-compatible nutrition regimens and the three static metabolic types

REGIMENS	METABOLIC TYPES		
	Acid	Mixed	Alkaline
Acid Compatible	❖		
Mixed Compatible		❖	
Alkaline Compatible			❖

❖ **BioBalance = Complete Biocompatibility** = Optimal Wellness. Clearly, only diagonal entries represent precise matches of nutritional regimens with metabolic types, due to the structure of the chart.

Partial Mismatch = Some Bio-Incompatibility = Noticeable deterioration of wellness over the longer term. This occurs when an acid type is matched with a mixed regimen or vice versa, because these categories are related but not identical

Significant Mismatch = Significant Bio-Incompatibility = Substantial deterioration of wellness over the short term. Occurs when an alkaline type is matched with a mixed regimen and vice versa. These two are almost, but not completely opposed.

Total Mismatch = Complete Bio-Incompatibility = Severe and rapid deterioration of wellness. The nutritional regimen aggravates the underlying imbalance bringing maximum inefficiency to metabolic processes at the cellular level.

For the sake of perspective, the columns have been sized to approximate the frequency of occurrence for each of the static metabolic types (60-75% alkaline; 13-15% acid; 13-15% mixed)

For simplicity's sake, cyclic metabolizers (about 10% of the population—mostly female) have been equally distributed and absorbed into the three columns of the static metabolic types

Row widths have been sized to approximate the tendency in the real world to favor fat/purine-rich diets within industrialized societies. The diets of industrialized societies are actually adulterated versions of the recommended or allowed foods within the acid-compatible and mixed-compatible regimens. This adulteration occurs through the prevalence of fast foods, processed foods, refined carbohydrates and rich desserts, etc.

In actual fact, cuisine favored by industrialized society is really a caricature of the acid-compatible and mixed-compatible regimens recommended as part of BioBalance Therapy. Industrialized society's caricatures include fast foods, processed foods, refined carbohydrates, rich desserts, etc. In any event, even in the idealized case represented in this matrix, the combined area encompassing both the upper right hand corner entry and the mid right hand entry is extremely large, reflecting the disproportionately high incidence of degenerative disease and (so-called) mental and behavioral disorders in industrialized societies. In the actual case (not shown in this matrix), adulteration of allowed foods within the acid-compatible and mixed compatible regimens, would penalize acid and mixed metabolizers, and deprive them of the full metabolic benefits they would otherwise receive

This matrix is especially enlightening since it cross-correlates the following three variables: 1. your metabolic type; 2. your eating habits; and, 3. your predicted wellness level. Consequently, this matrix is actually a legible or easy-to-read three-dimensional graph.

At this point, you should be able to understand why an across-the-board application of "light fare/light cuisine" (as suggested by the mainstream dietary community) would simply favor alkaline metabolizers at the expense of all other metabolizers. Admittedly, alkaline metabolizers do form the majority population (as illustrated by column width in the matrix), but I have already shown you why the mainstream nutritional community need not continue playing the non-discriminating and sometimes destructive zero-sum-game of robbing Peter (acid metabolizers) to give to Paul (alkaline metabolizers) which it has been playing for the past 30+ years, and which it shows no sign abandoning.

This matrix also shows you at a glance why there is so much confusion, chaos and contradiction in the field of nutrition and holistic or alternative health care. Clearly, absent an understanding of BioBalance Therapy, the probability of randomly selecting a diet, which is capable of yielding consistently good results, is small.

In essence, the following chain of events has unfolded within the health care community. Any given nutritional or holistic expert has had both good and bad therapeutic outcomes with a particular diet. *It is all too tempting for the expert in question to ascribe poor outcomes to the patient's unwillingness to follow through with the diet in question.* Worse still, the patient is blamed when the health care provider claims that the diet's failure is the result of "deep-seated emotional problems." The health care provider will then claim that these problems will require follow-up "intensive probing by a sensitive and certified/qualified psychotherapist," or "a skilled stress management specialist."

In many regards, the ongoing saga of the almost comedic chaos in nutrition today is akin to the fable of the blind men and the elephant. In essence, this story describes the argument which ensues among a number of wise but blind men in attempting to discuss the nature of an elephant. The blind man grasping its tail claims the elephant is like a rope. The blind man grasping its ear claims the elephant is like a fan. The blind man grasping its side claims the elephant is like a wall. The blind man grasping its trunk claims the elephant is like a snake. The blind man grasping its tusk claims that the elephant is like a spear. The blind man grasping its leg claims that the elephant is like a tree . . . and so on. Each blind man in turn claims that the other blind men are wrong.

Analogously, each so-called holistic and nutritional expert today is one of the blind men, and the acid/alkaline spectrum of human metabolic diversity is the elephant. Each so-called expert claims complete knowledge after grasping only one part of that spectrum, and vociferously resorts to name-calling and character assassinations claiming that anyone with a contradictory view is wrong or "a quack."

You can readily see that while this type of debate may make good talk-show material it adds nothing to our understanding of the human condition. On a recent talk-show, one internationally acclaimed "expert" boldly proclaimed that so varied a set of nutritional outcomes could only mean that nutrition had little to do with health, but meant instead that the individual's *belief* in the power of a particular diet was the over-riding factor in determining whether that diet would succeed or fail. He of course felt that his personal blend of psychotherapy and New Age mysticism was the answer. In other words, this expert would rather have you believe that the elephant is an illusion, than allow you to conclude that *metabolic diversity* is the reason why outcomes are varied. Don't laugh. You'd be shocked by this individual's enormous name recognition potential, the thunderous applause his comment received (no less than a standing ovation), and the subsequent adoration heaped upon him both by the talk-show host and audience - yet another "box office sensation." Popular culture is clearly plummeting to new depths of superstition.

The illustration below depicts in cartoon form the summary narrative I've just provided of the children's fable of *The Blind Men and the Elephant.* Tables 1 & 2 on pages 31 and 32 list the predictable success rates of BioBalance Therapy compared to its competition. Given the fact that you now understand the far-reaching implications of human metabolic diversity, you can see why BioBalance Therapy can be successful when other, more commercial programs cannot.

No, BioBalance is not THE final answer, but it is a scientifically founded answer that sheds considerable light on a huge part of the food-mood-health puzzle, which will *never* be understood until we all understand the implications of human acid/alkaline intermediary metabolic diversity. In another sense, the quandary the health care community is in today is much like the quandary astronomy was in prior to Isaac Newton's time. Thousands of astronomers were mesmerized and enthralled by the concept of planetary and solar *epicycles* which they inherited from the ancients. These *epicyclic schemes* which were "box office sensations" in their own day, became increasingly bizarre and complex as part of feverish and futile attempts to understand the motion of the planets and sun; (orbits within orbits within orbits maintained by invisible extra-terrestrials possessing super-human strength, etc..) In the end, it turned out that the following three profound, but very simple concepts replaced the countless epicyclic schemes required to interpret thousands of apparently unrelated pieces of the planetary motion puzzle:

• the sun is the center of the solar system
• the law of gravity
• the laws of motion (as articulated by "the mathematics of variations" or the calculus)

As history demonstrated, the established professional community's first response to these three simple principles was one of disbelief. After all, how could phenomena as complex as planetary motion (indeed, the very "motion of the heavens themselves") be reduced to so simple a set of principles? Furthermore, how could the senses be deceived into believing that the earth and planets revolved around the sun, when it was clear that the sun moved daily around the earth? You can see why the so-called experts in astronomy contemporary with Galileo and Newton felt smug in asserting that anyone who accepted the three principles outlined above was a heretic or a simpleton (i.e., "politically incorrect," or a fool).

With the benefit of history's 20/20 hindsight we can see who had the last laugh. As truth was ultimately uncovered, thousands of complex and arcane aspects of epicyclic planetary motion become recognized as foolishness.

One wonders how much longer it will take, and how much more needless suffering the public will have to endure before the simplicity of BioBalance Therapy is accepted by today's professionals and integrated into standard medical care.

Let me reiterate, it should be clear to you by now that BioBalance Therapy does not merely apply to "sick people, fat people and/or crazy people," (people who have disorders commonly and erroneously classified as "mental"). Since *everyone's* health and behavior are to a significant extent driven by intermediary metabolic activity, *no one is immune to the principles of BioBalance Therapy*. Consequently, it would be entirely appropriate for the medical community to *universally* integrate BioBalance Therapy into standard medical care. This statement is true despite the fact that you can determine your BioProfile and implement BioBalance Therapy without medical assistance.

Indeed, as I explain in the final chapter, BioBalance Therapy should be *the first diagnostic tool used by every medical practitioner* irrespective of his/her specialty. Why? Because the application of BioBalance Therapy is the scientific way to bolster your intermediary metabolic activity (and hence your *immune system*), thereby enhancing the probability of success of any subsequent medical treatment you may undergo for any given illness. Similarly, long-term adherence to BioBalance Therapy should lessen the probability of your falling victim to illnesses to which you might otherwise fall victim in the absence of BioBalance Therapy, whether you are genetically predisposed to that illness or not. BioBalance Therapy is effective both in helping you to *prevent* illness, and in *lessening the severity and/or longevity* of an ongoing illness

Lastly, unlike my first book, this book avoids lengthy discussions of emotionally and politically charged issues (such as the debatable effectiveness of psychotherapy, and some of the shortcomings of mainstream and alternative health care). Those issues are touched on very briefly in this book's final chapter. My personal feelings or your personal feelings regarding those issues are really irrelevant. The critical point is this: BioBalance Therapy is based upon rigorously derived scientific principles, and not upon the placebo effect commonly known as the power of suggestion. ***In other words, you need not believe in BioBalance Therapy in order for it to succeed. All you need do is apply it.***

Table 1 — BioBalance Therapy's Effectiveness

Applicable to - All BioProfiles. Success rate = 90%+, itemized as follows:

65%-to-75%+ = complete recovery

25%-to-15%+ = partial remission

less than 10% = no improvement

These success rates improve if the premier nutritional regimens listed in chapter 2 are applied.

Table 2 — How the Diets and the Doctor Diets Stack Up

Author	Regimen	Compatible BioProfile & Success Rate
M. Kushi	Macrobiotics	alkaline 75%

In all fairness, because of macrobiotics' high success rate, macrobiotics is in a league of its own. The reason why macrobiotics' success rate is so high as compared with the success rates of all the other nutritional regimens (below) is discussed in chapter 2. I would urge you to read that chapter carefully since it details each of the 3 premier reformulated variations of each of the 3 nutritional regimens discussed thus far. By implementing the information in the next chapter you will further enhance the probability of BioBalance Therapy's success.

Author	Regimen	Compatible BioProfile & Success Rate
R. Atkins	The Super Energy Diet also more recently called "Ketogenics"	acid<->mixed < 25%
B. Sears	The Zone	acid<->mixed < 25%
P. D'Adamo	Eat Right for Your Type	too varied to permit evaluation
S. Berger	The Immune Power Diet	some alkaline < 25%
Ringsdorf & Cheraskin	Psychodietetics	variable but typically some alkaline < 25%
R. Norris	The PMS Diet	some alkaline < 25%

Table 2 *(continued)*

Author	Regimen	Compatible BioProfile & Success Rate
W. Crook	Anticandida	acid<->mixed < 25%
O. Truss	Anticandida	acid<->mixed < 25%
B. Feingold	Antihyperkinesis	too varied to permit evaluation
T. Randolph	Hypoallergenic	too varied to permit Elimination/Rotation evaluation
J. Wurtman	High Complex Carbohydrate Diets	alkaline < 25%
A. Weil	Dr. Weil's application of nutrition within the context of holistic/ complementary health care	too varied to permit evaluation
N. Pritikin	Pritikin Program	alkaline < 25%
R. Haas	Eat to Win/Eat to Succeed	alkaline < 25%
Harvey & Marilyn Diamond	Fit for Life	alkaline < 25%
W. Wolcott & T. Fahey	Metabolic Typing Diet	arbitrary correlations have little to do with metabolic activity

Chapter

2

The Premier Nutritional Regimens:
Macrobiotics and its Nutritional Opposite

Why is macrobiotics' success rate (75%) disproportionately higher than the success rate of the other nutritional regimens listed at the end of the previous chapter? I'll answer this question in this chapter. In so doing I'll tell you why I feel that macrobiotics is the premier nutritional regimen for alkaline metabolizers (and *alkaline metabolizers only*), and why I recommend it as the premier nutritional regimen of choice for all alkaline metabolizers, especially for those suffering from degenerative disease, irrespective of whether they elect additional allopathic (mainstream medical) treatment or not. I'll then go on to outline an ideal nutritional regimen for mixed and acid metabolizers.

It would be impossible for me to do macrobiotics full justice in the short a space this chapter allows. I will attempt to discuss macrobiotics in brief, giving you a short summary of its dietary guidelines. I purposely choose the word "guidelines" since macrobiotic advisors claim that a macrobiotic regimen must be tailor-made for each individual. My observations suggest that the extent of variability which macrobiotics claims may, to a large extent, be artifact and superfluous. So, the guidelines I list below suggest a core diet or regimen.

The word "macrobiotics" has as its roots the Greek words *macro* and *bio*, meaning "great" or "all-inclusive," and "life" or "life force" respectively. While macrobiotics is not a religion, macrobiotic dietary practices were derived from Buddhist theology approximately 2,400 years ago which advocates—even today—nonviolence to all living things. I hasten to add that macrobiotics is religion-neutral. One may subscribe to any (or no) institutionalized religion, and still adhere to macrobiotic dietary practices. Eating in macrobiotic fashion does not make one a Buddhist. I know of more than a few devout Christians, Jews, Moslems, Hindus and Buddhists who are "macrobiotic." Conversely, there are also Buddhists who do not adhere to macrobiotic dietary practices.

Religion aside, macrobiotic dietary principles were first recorded 2400 years ago by Asian physicians practicing in what is now Japan, China and the northern portion of the Indian sub-continent. By way of very brief review (references are included at the end of this book), macrobiotics' main dietary thrust consists of devising nutritional regimens, which strive to keep the individual's life force or *chi* (pronounced "chee") in balance. This life force is considered to be in continuous dynamic equilibrium as a result of the two primary countervailing forces which it embodies and which are hypothesized to exist in all nature, namely the forces of *yin* and *yang* (pronounced "yeen" and "yahng," respectively). These forces are *complementary antagonists* or *necessary opposites*, and are required to off-set each other to achieve *dynamic equilibrium*. In this context, disease is viewed as a disequilibriation or imbalance in life force as a result of excessive yin or yang. Some examples of yin and yang are: female and male, passivity and activity, cold and heat, etc. Macrobiotics stresses that nothing is purely yin or yang, but some combination of the two, and that every individual requires the presence of both yin and yang to maintain a state of dynamic equilibrium described by small amplitude oscillations about an equilibrium or balance point.

According to macrobiotic philosophy, dynamic equilibrium (as opposed to static equilibrium - no oscillation about a balance point) is emphasized since static equilibrium is virtually impossible to achieve. Consequently, every individual's chi can and should be expected to oscillate to some degree about its respective balance point in the yin-yang spectrum. The amplitudes of these oscillations are relatively small in healthy individuals, characterizing a state of relative dynamic balance. Conversely, these amplitudes will be relatively large in diseased individuals. Worse yet, in the severely diseased individual large oscillations will occur around a point in the yin-yang spectrum, which is not at its center.

Some macrobiotic practitioners in the 20th century suggest that acid and alkaline are also respective examples of yin and yang. As this chapter will demonstrate, this hypothesis may have considerable merit.

Nevertheless, further discussion about the nature of yin and yang is not necessary in furthering our understanding of the role which macrobiotics plays in BioBalance Therapy. It suffices to say that foods are also endowed with yin and yang qualities, and macrobiotics' goal is to have the individual eat foods whose yin/yang properties situate them close to the center of the yin/yang spectrum thereby imparting a more balanced life force to the individual.

The discoveries made by macrobiotic practitioners via trial-and-error approximately 2,400 years ago are somewhat remarkable as you shall soon see. Trial-and-error in determining whether a food was appropriate or inappropriate was necessary, since modern understandings of biochemistry and metabolism did not exist at the time macrobiotics got its start. The trial-and-error approach of that day consisted simply of having a practitioner (typically a physician in a royal court or a monk) fast for several days, then ingest one and only one food, and then subjectively record its effect upon him. A glance at the guidelines listed below shows the remarkable similarity between the allowed core macrobiotic regimen and the regimen listed in BioBalance Therapy as appropriate for alkaline types. I'll tell you why this similarity is not an accident. Once again, these guidelines are simply an illustration of a core macrobiotic regimen.

Macrobiotic Dietary Guidelines

(Note: Most specialty items included herein may be purchased at health food stores and/or macrobiotic food outlets – see references)

WHOLE GRAINS:

PRIMARY - short grain brown rice, millet and barley
SECONDARY - all other whole grains such as medium grain brown rice, buckwheat, wheat, whole oats, quinoa (pronounced "keen-wah"), amaranth, corn, teff, etc. (Some of these grains were not of course indigenous to Asia at the time macrobiotics was conceived, but were introduced later from Europe and the Americas); whole grain pastas, whole grain breads, preferably made with sprouted whole grains and devoid of flour (commonly referred to in today's market as Essene or Ezekiel breads).

Ideally almost 100% of the breakfast meal should consist of whole grains, while 50%-to-60% of each of the lunch and dinner meals should consist of whole grains.

VEGETABLES:

PRIMARY - carrots, broccoli, broccoli raabe, pumpkin-like squashes such as Hokkaido pumpkin, acorn squash, butternut squash, etc., radishes especially daikon radish, onions including scallions and leeks, kale, mustard greens, collards, parsnips, rutabagas, turnips, burdock roots, lotus roots, brussel sprouts, cabbage especially bok choy cabbage, and sea vegetables.

SECONDARY - legumes (beans, peas and lentils) of any variety especially aduki beans, garbanzo beans and lentils, tofu, chestnuts, certain mushrooms, especially shitake mushrooms.

USE SPARINGLY or IDEALLY AVOID COMPLETELY - artichokes and artichoke hearts, asparagus, spinach, cauliflower, all other mushrooms, peanuts, all other nuts and seeds, nightshades (peppers, eggplants, tomatoes, potatoes - including sweet potatoes and yams); nightshades should typically be used sparingly or avoided by individuals with bone and joint problems and degenerative diseases.

Ideally, 35%-to-25% of each of the lunch and dinner meals should consist of a combination of the primary vegetables (with the exception of legumes), and 15% of each of these meals should consist of legumes especially aduki beans, garbanzo beans and lentils.

FRUITS:

All fruits—even the primary ones listed below—should be eaten only in season and eaten sparingly.

PRIMARY - apples, pears, peaches, apricots, berries, cherries, plums, melons, and typically all fruits which macrobiotics classifies as "northern fruits."

USE SPARINGLY or IDEALLY AVOID COMPLETELY - avocados, bananas, grapes, and all tropical fruits (such as citrus, etc.), fruit jams and jellies (despite the fact that jams and jellies may be "all natural" and devoid of added sugars or additives).

ANIMAL FOODS:

All animal foods—even the primary ones listed below—should be eaten in moderation if not sparingly (not more than 2 to 3 meals per week, and not more than 3-to-4 ounces per meal for the primaries, and only in small quantities on festive occasions for the secondaries).

PRIMARY - cod, scrod, carp or light meat trout
SECONDARY - shrimp and scallops
AVOID - all other animal foods

DAIRY and EGGS:

Egg yolks may be used on rare occasions only to treat certain types of *rare* disorders (not discussed herein), but dairy and eggs should otherwise be avoided completely.

BEVERAGES:

PRIMARY - tea made by steeping the branches and twigs of the kukicha or bancha bush in hot water (but not leaves since this bush's leaves have a high caffeine content); tea made by steeping roasted whole grains (primarily short grain brown rice, barley and millet) in hot water
SECONDARY - tea made by steeping roasted dandelion roots in hot water; 0% alcohol beer
USE SPARINGLY – unsweetened soy milk (or very lightly sweetened with rice syrup or barley syrup/malt); soy/fruit frappe (with allowed fruits only); all other decaffeinated and relatively innocuous herbal teas, beer, rice wine or sake
AVOID - all other beverages especially, colas, tea, coffee (both caffeinated and decaffeinated), soft drinks, wines and liquors

CONDIMENTS:

The references I provide list the various macrobiotic condiments which may be used and the extent to which they may be used. I will not list them here since they are not essential to this discussion.

METHODS of PREPARATION:

PREFERRED - heat sources should consist of natural gas; methods of preparation include water sautéing, blanching, boiling, pressure cooking, steaming, stir frying in very small amounts of toasted sesame seed oil (meant to impart flavor and prevent foods from sticking rather than to add any significant amount of added dietary fat). Cooking utensils (especially pots and pans) should ideally be made of cast iron, stainless steel, and/or heat treated glass, and not synthetics (such as Teflon, plastic, etc.) or aluminum.

USE SPARINGLY on FESTIVE OCCASIONS ONLY, and for INDIVIDUALS WHO ARE RELATIVELY FREE of ILLNESS - frying (using toasted sesame seed oil only). With the exception of olive oil which may be used in very small quantities to add flavor to some foods, most other added oils and fats are to be used sparingly, and animal fats such as lard, chicken fat, duck/goose fat, etc. are to be avoided completely.

So, by way of quick review, breakfast consists of whole grains only. Lunch consists of *miso* soup or broth - pronounced meeso - (warm water with dissolved miso paste - miso is a fermented whole grain and soy product), 50%-to-60% whole grains, 35%-to-25% primary vegetables, and 15% legumes, and a primary beverage (typically kukicha tea). Dinner may differ from lunch, but should have similar proportions of food types as lunch. Occasionally (2 to 3 times per week), allowed seafood may be added to the lunch or dinner meal, but typically not at both lunch an dinner.

Needless to say, this is a simplification of the many meals and modes of preparation used within the macrobiotic dietary framework, but it provides a quick-look at this highly successful nutritional therapy in treating alkaline metabolizers. With few exceptions, it is clear that the core macrobiotic regimen is strikingly similar to a critical subset of the regimen appropriate for alkaline metabolizers. There are some notable exceptions which I will discuss shortly, but let me first answer a more important question, namely why is macrobiotics so successful?

- First and foremost, 75% of the male population is alkaline, and 60% of the female population is alkaline all the time, while another 10% of the female population is alkaline for some if not most of the time (cyclic BioProfiles which are characterized by the alkaline state as one part of the cycle). Because much of the population of Asia subsisted on grains and vegetables when macrobiotics was devised approximately 2400 years ago, it's my guess that these percentages were even higher because of natural selection. Specifically, the relative scarcity of foods appropriate for nonalkaline metabolizers (such as red meats, organ meats, shell fish and crustaceans, and certain vegetables, etc.) would have logically led to the early/untimely death of a disproportionate percentage of nonalkaline (acid and mixed) metabolizers. The relative scarcity of foods appropriate for nonalkaline metabolizers also would have made surviving nonalkaline metabolizers mentally and behaviorally maladaptive. Consequently, nonalkaline metabolizers never had a biological or behavioral advantage in competition with their alkaline counterparts, and were thus likely barred entry into the monastic and physician class. Nonalkaline metabolizers, therefore, rarely participated in acting as "midwives" in the birth of macrobiotics. The overwhelming majority of monks/physicians participating in the aforementioned trial-and-error process were almost certainly alkaline metabolizers who responded well to most of those foods listed as appropriate for alkaline metabolizers, and responded poorly to those foods listed as inappropriate for alkaline metabolizers.
- Admittedly, there are some paradoxical occurrences where macrobiotics is at odds with BioBalance Therapy. Specifically, macrobiotics excludes low fat dairy, eggs, tropical fruits, nightshades, and coffee, while including legumes (beans, peas and lentils). At second glance, these apparent paradoxes may be resolved as follows:

A. **DAIRY and EGGS:** 2400 years ago, dairy always consisted of whole dairy, not low fat dairy. Whole dairy is considered inappropriate for alkaline types even by BioBalance Therapy's standards today. Why? Because the fat content of whole dairy (as is true of all fats) is highly alkaline-inducing. It drives venous plasma pH up. Furthermore, dairy (even low fat dairy) and eggs are not hypoallergenic. It is therefore possible that adverse reactions to these foods in macrobiotics' trial-and-error screening process were provoked by allergic reactions and/or gastrointestinal problems (lactose intolerance), in addition to reactions resulting from metabolic incompatibility. When you are screening foods via trial-and-error, an adverse reaction is an adverse reaction, since you are unable to differentiate whether that reaction is metabolic, allergic or candida-provoking in nature. For this reason, these foods were quickly excluded during the macrobiotic trial-and-error development process.

B. **FRUITS:** Most tropical fruits are candida-inducing. Once again, when you are screening foods via trial-and-error, an adverse reaction is an adverse reaction, since you are unable to differentiate whether that reaction is metabolic, allergic or candida-provoking in nature.

C. **LEGUMES** (beans, peas and lentils): It's my guess that legumes were initially screened out by macrobiotic practitioners. However, it soon became apparent that a macrobiotic regimen devoid of legumes led to muscle and organ wasting and ultimately starvation and death. The biochemical reason for this event results from the fact that there is not enough seafood in macrobiotics to supply the individual with all of the essential amino acids to sustain and regenerate organ and muscle mass. Recall that Buddhist theology espouses nonviolence to all living things. Consequently, the ingestion of seafood (which contains all of the essential amino acids sufficient to permit muscle and organ regeneration) was likely viewed as a taboo. A small quantity of legumes (about 15% by volume) complemented with a large amount of whole grains will, however, provide the individual with all of the essential amino acids and will resolve this problem. So, once again, astute observation as part of the trial-and-error process permitted small quantities of legumes. It is not an accident that macrobiotic literature is replete with warnings to the reader to refrain from eating too many legumes. Specifically, one of the macrobiotic movement's 20th century leaders, George Oshawa has gone on record to state, "A man who eats too many legumes will become a fool." This statement is not absurd when it is interpreted within the context of BioBalance Therapy and macrobiotics' biocompatibility with alkaline metabolizers.

D. **NIGHTSHADES:** Nightshades are allowed for alkaline metabolizers, yet macrobiotic advisors suggest that they be used sparingly if at all by healthy individuals, and avoided by individuals suffering degenerative disorders, especially those disorders impacting bones and joints. Most if not all the nightshades were discovered in the Americas in the late 15th and early 16th century. Consequently, they were unknown when macrobiotics was first being developed. Nonetheless, these foods were still discouraged when they were introduced to Asia.

More than a few of BioBalance Therapy's more observant patients suffering from arthritis and related disorders routinely report that the nightshades do, in fact, result in increased pain. In all honesty, I don't know why this is the case. I can't chalk these unwanted side effects up to candidiasis or gastroenteritis. But if we assume that the trial-and-error method employed by macrobiotic physicians also elicited similar responses, we can see why these foods were viewed as unacceptable. A clearer understanding of how these foods impact the skeletal system, and in particular osteoclast and osteoblast activity (destruction and regeneration of bone respectively) is required before any definitive statements can be made.

E. **COFFEE:** Coffee was not widely known in Asia at the time macrobiotics was developed. In any event, conventional teas made from any one of a variety of tea leaves had been discovered and were widely used. However, the trial-and-error process consisted of having a monk or physician ingest a specific food after several days of fasting, and fasting for so long a period of time is usually acid-inducing. It is therefore highly likely that even a modest amount of caffeine (commonly found in tea) pushed the subject's fasting metabolism into a transient and severe state of acidosis which, in turn, produced significant discomfort even for an alkaline metabolizer. Consequently, regular tea (with caffeine) was disqualified by the macrobiotic community as would have been the case for coffee had it been consumed as well. If you are alkaline, and you try this experiment as I have, you will find that my hypothesis is correct.

We are thus left with a subset of a diet appropriate for alkaline metabolizers, which also includes a *small amount* of legumes required to prevent starvation resulting from essential amino acid insufficiency. Large quantities of legumes are inappropriate for alkaline types. This generalized, core macrobiotic diet has a few advantages over the easier-to-follow (and more inclusive) alkaline-appropriate regimen I list in this book and in my first book, as follows:

- The core macrobiotic nutritional regimen's nucleoprotein or purine composition is extremely low. As I already mentioned in chapter 1, nucleoproteins (also known as purines) are those proteins that cause an individual's intermediary metabolism to shift into a relatively alkaline mode. By way of review, nucleoproteins or purines are found in abundance in foods appropriate for acid and mixed mode metabolizers. This is precisely why these foods are to be avoided by alkaline metabolizers. Legumes (peas, beans and lentils) ingested in *small quantities* are the only exception to this rule, and this exception has already been explained.
- The core macrobiotic nutritional regimen discourages the addition of fats. By modern standards, the caloric content provided by fats in the core macrobiotic regimen is approximately 15%. As is the case with nucleoproteins, fats are also alkaline-inducing, and should thus be used sparingly by alkaline metabolizers. A zero fat diet will of course ultimately lead to serious health problems and death. The fats in the macrobiotic regimen are naturally contained in the recommended foods.

- The core macrobiotic nutritional regimen is very high in fiber, thus keeping bowel movements regular, and ridding the body of toxins.
- The core macrobiotic nutritional regimen is lacking in most if not all hyper-allergenic foods, candida-provoking foods, and foods which may trigger gastro-intestinal upset.

Consequently, macrobiotics helps *alkaline metabolizers* achieve a strong state of BioBalance without provoking undesirable side effects such as candidiasis, allergic reactions and gastro-intestinal upset. All of this speaks very highly of the macrobiotic regimen *when applied to alkaline metabolizers only,* and illustrates why macrobiotics is so successful. Couple this with the fact that the majority—approximately 75%—of any given population consists of alkaline metabolizers, and it is little wonder that macrobiotics provides so many testimonials in resolving a broad spectrum of problems ranging from the so-called "psychological" problems at one end of the disease spectrum to life threatening degenerative disorders such as terminal cancer at the other.

There is a saying that when your only weapon is a hammer, you will treat the world as though it were a nail. In this regard, and on the downside, the macrobiotic community believes that there is a macrobiotic regimen that can be tailor-made for anyone. Given your familiarity with basic BioBalance Therapy, you can see why it is difficult if not impossible to substantiate this claim. Indeed, it is my counter-claim that a significant minority (approximately 25%) of any given population's symptoms (the nonalkaline minority) will be aggravated by a diet similar to the macrobiotic regimen. It would be a tragic error to simply discount these failures due to extra-metabolic factors (i.e., perhaps their problems "really" are psychological, or perhaps, their problems have nothing to do with nutrition, and metabolism, etc.).

Yes, there are problems which are extra-nutritional, but if we focus upon that class of problems or diseases which are commonly classified as stress-related, psychological. psychogenic or "mental," we consistently find that most of these disorders have a very predictable nutritional/metabolic component. Because intermediary metabolic activity is intimately tied to immune system activity, it is also not unreasonable to conclude that similar statements may be made regarding other forms of illness as well. Furthermore, as discussed in this book's final chapter, it is extremely unlikely that "talking things over with a qualified and sensitive expert" will help at all. (Again, this statement is backed up by double blind placebo trials, and is not simply my opinion.)

At any rate, given that you've come this far in your understanding of BioBalance Therapy, you can see why attempts to blame the patient for a failure of the therapy is dishonest. The *real* reason why macrobiotics is strikingly successful in treating a majority of the population, but not so for a 25% minority, stems from the fact that we humans are metabolically diverse, and macrobiotics is metabolically incompatible only with nonalkaline (acid and mixed) metabolic types.

The question we are now faced with is whether it is possible to devise nutritional regimens compatible with nonalkaline metabolizers which also offer all of the other benefits offered by macrobiotics. The answer to this question is yes, and detailed descriptions of these regimens are outlined below.

Devising the nutritional, acid/alkaline opposite of the macrobiotic regimen consists of modifying the regimen to include nucleoprotein-rich or purine-rich seafood and vegetables. Further modifications can be made to create ideal regimens for both acid and mixed metabolizers. Unlike the case of macrobiotics, it is advisable for nonalkaline metabolizers to eat seafood to a greater extent than their macrobiotic alkaline counterparts. Since purine-rich seafood has far higher concentrations of purines than purine-rich vegetables, it is inadvisable for nonalkaline types to attempt to fully replace purine-rich seafood with purine-rich vegetables. Recall that the nucleoprotein or purine component of food is that component which causes your metabolism to shift toward the alkaline end of the spectrum (it drives venous plasma pH up), thus relieving or counter-effecting an underlying acid imbalance.

Examples of fish and seafood which are rich in nucleoprotein/ purine are: salmon (both red and pink), dark meat tuna (*not* fancy white albacore), darker meat fish in general (bluefish, steel-head trout, sardines, herrings, etc.), shellfish such as clams, oysters and scallops, crustaceans such as shrimp, lobsters and crayfish.

Examples of vegetables which contain moderate amounts of nucleoprotein/purine are: spinach, asparagus, cauliflower, artichokes and artichoke hearts, mushrooms, and legumes (peas, beans and lentils of any variety plus peanuts, nuts and seeds).

Whole grains contain very little nucleoprotein/purine, but are absolutely essential in detoxifying the body and maintaining normal bowel function. Consequently, whole grain consumption (in moderation) should be included at every meal. Unlike the case where alkaline metabolizers are concerned, nonalkaline metabolizers should avoid whole grain pasta or use it sparingly. Needless to say, all processed foods should be avoided.

Ideally, all dairy and eggs should be avoided since they lack nucleoprotein, and do little if anything to neutralize the acid metabolic imbalance, which characterizes the intermediary metabolic activity of both acid and mixed mode metabolizers.

Added fat (which may occasionally exceed the 10%-to-15% level appropriate for alkaline metabolizers) should ideally be added via extra virgin, cold pressed olive oil. Since purine-rich seafood forms the core of the regimens appropriate for nonalkaline types, these metabolizers need not add much fat to their regimens since the amount of hidden fat beneficial to their metabolic types is included in these foods. Stir-frying in modest amounts of oil is allowed.

Fruit should be used sparingly. On those occasions when fruit is eaten, it should consist of so-called northern fruit as well as bananas and avocados, whereas all other tropical fruits (especially citrus) should be avoided.

Beverages should ideally exclude all caffeinated beverages, similar to the beverages allowed by macrobiotics.

A description of a sample macrobiotic breakfast, lunch and dinner appropriate for alkaline metabolizers has already been listed. A description of a sample breakfast, lunch and dinner appropriate for acid metabolizers who wish to refrain from eating animal foods higher up the food chain than seafood is now outlined below.

- **BREAKFAST:** Modest portion of any whole grain (or steel cut oats on occasion) supplemented with a primary seafood (such as kippers - popular in British and Celtic cultures). Note that acid metabolizers must ingest allowed animal protein at every meal. Some mixed metabolizers report that they do not require animal protein for breakfast, but must eat it for both lunch and dinner. These mixed metabolizers should *not* be misclassified as diurnal cyclers. They are not. They may eat in relatively "light" fashion for breakfast, but must eat in heavier fashion for both lunch and dinner. Once again, the only way to determine whether you are a mixed metabolizer requiring light or heavy fare for breakfast involves trial-and-error. As stated in Chapter One, the caffeine test is used to determine whether you are alkaline or nonalkaline.

- **LUNCH:** Miso soup or broth as previously described, 15%-to-25% whole grains, 15%-to-25% primary vegetables, 25% legumes, and the remainder (25%+) would consist of primary seafood. (All percentages are given in terms of volume or plate area size.) Lunch should also include a primary beverage, typically kukicha tea.

- **DINNER:** Dinner may differ from lunch in content, but it is formally similar to lunch.

Unlike alkaline types, *acid metabolizers must eat some purine-rich food at every meal,* including breakfast, otherwise their purine intake will be too low to enable them to offset the acid imbalance to which their metabolism is naturally prone. I recommend that acid metabolizers rely upon a generous bowl of rich homemade legume soup with miso and modestly seasoned with cold-pressed extra-virgin olive oil in addition, of course, to purine-rich fish or seafood. This type of soup along with primary seafood and vegetables should provide an excellent counterbalance to an underlying acid disorder.

Mixed mode metabolizers should eat in a mixed fashion appropriate for both acid and alkaline metabolizers, biasing their fare in favor of those foods appropriate for acid metabolizers in an approximate ratio of 2:1 (acid metabolizer compatible = the "heavy diet": alkaline metabolizer compatible = the "light diet"), to as much as 4:1 depending upon the severity of their metabolic imbalance.

Mixed mode metabolizers should recall that if they err, they are better off erring in favor of a "heavier" regimen than a "lighter" regimen, since their metabolic imbalance resembles that of acid metabolizers far more than that of alkaline metabolizers. Many mixed mode metabolizers (approximately 50%) find that they may even skip eating purine-rich animal protein for breakfast with impunity, but they *must* eat purine-rich animal protein for *both lunch and dinner.* In other words, breakfast for individuals within this class of mixed mode metabolizers may consist of relatively light to medium fare (which excludes purine-rich seafood or more generally purine-rich animal food), but they *must* introduce purine-rich seafood and purine-rich vegetables for lunch. Other mixed mode metabolizers find that they *must* eat purine-rich seafood (or more generally, purine-rich animal protein) for breakfast. Fine-tuning of this nature depends upon the mixed mode individual, and is typically accomplished via straightforward short-term trial and error. This issue is discussed in additional detail later.

Finally, after a person has determined his/her metabolic type and has settled upon his/her biocompatible regimen, (s)he may then introduce the appropriate companion vitamin/mineral supplement. Once again, you must be certain of your metabolic BioProfile, and be certain that you have engaged your appropriate nutritional regimen(s) before you initiate vitamin/mineral therapy. In the event that you do not respond well to your supplements (even though they may be appropriate for you), do not take the supplements, but do continue with your regimen(s). *Remember, the largest extent of your recovery is attributed to your nutritional regimen.*

I realize that a good portion of the seafood appropriate for nonalkaline types is marketed in tins or cans. While I would recommend fresh food and preferably organic food and produce, I also realize that some choices are limited and unavoidable. If you are nonalkaline and feel that you must have more diversity in your diet, you may eat dark meat fowl and poultry, but I would urge you to purchase hormone-free, antibiotic-free, free ranging poultry which has been organically fed. While BioBalance Therapy focuses upon human health, I am concerned about conditions under which food animals are raised, for two reasons:

• The long term repercussions upon human health of the food additives, hormones and antibiotics given to animals are at best questionable.

• Animals should be spared as much suffering as possible whenever possible. Frankly, I feel it's hypocritical of us to create a double standard in treating our pets with kindness and affection, and then employ another standard in the treatment of livestock. Nevertheless, it's far beyond the scope of this book to engage in a dialogue dealing with the ethical treatment of animals, and where to draw the line in seeking an equitable trade-off between human health and the ethical treatment of animals.

I therefore urge all metabolic types to do the following:

- First use the entire set of biocompatible animal foods in counter-effecting your metabolic imbalance(s), making sure to use animal protein derived from organically fed, hormone-free and additive-free livestock in order to avoid unwanted side effects.

- After you have accurately determined your BioProfile, and you have counter-effected your metabolic imbalance(s), you should strive to restrict your core animal food intake to fish and seafood, and (if necessary) to your biocompatible meat (white vs. dark) derived from organically fed, naturally raised, additive-free, hormone-free, free-ranging poultry only.

In the case of alkaline metabolizers, the second recommendation above is tantamount to adhering to a macrobiotic regimen. In the case of nonalkaline metabolizers, this second recommendation is tantamount to adhering to one or both of macrobiotics' opposing regimen(s) discussed above. The probability is high that alkaline metabolizers will feel a significant if not substantial improvement in adhering to macrobiotics over the standard regimen appropriate for alkaline metabolizers. On the other hand, if nonalkaline metabolizers find that they simply cannot achieve the same degree of BioBalance (and wellness) by eating nucleoprotein/purine-rich seafood, they should simply adhere to the standard nutritional regimens appropriate for nonalkaline types. When they do include allowed/primary animal foods in their diet, they should always try to select those which are organically fed, hormone-free, and free ranging. In the final analysis, as much as I am aware of the need to protect our animal friends, in the contest between animal rights and human rights, priority must be given to humans while simultaneously giving animals the most humane treatment possible.

Chapter

3

Your Personal Metabolic Makeover

You are now ready to determine your BioProfile, and in so doing select your biocompatible nutritional regimen(s). In Chapter One I stated that there is one over-riding factor, which is generally reliable in determining your BioProfile, namely your caffeine tolerance. (Hereinafter, all references to coffee mean only regular, non-decaffeinated coffee.)

By way of quick review, how does the caffeine tolerance test work?

- **Alkaline metabolizers** almost always need at least one cup of coffee every morning to wake up and get started, and perhaps an occasional cup or more later in the day (especially either mid-morning and/or after lunch) either to stay awake, to re-energize or remain motivated. I've even worked with alkaline metabolizers who require a cup of coffee at night to help them relax, unwind and fall asleep. Note that I never recommend a high caffeine diet for any alkaline metabolizer irrespective of the severity of his/her underlying metabolic imbalance. In this regard, fine-tuning has demonstrated that as alkaline metabolizers achieve BioBalance, their need for caffeine typically drops to the point where they require very little if any coffee.
- **Acid metabolizers** generally cannot tolerate even a fraction of a cup of coffee. In fact, acid metabolizers can rarely tolerate colas or soft drinks containing caffeine.
- **Mixed metabolizers** will typically feel a little tense or nervous after drinking one cup of coffee or less (especially in the morning), and generally quite nervous after drinking more than 1 cup.

- Individuals who possess **Cyclic BioProfiles** (alkaline during certain well-defined time frames, and nonalkaline during others) typically find that their caffeine tolerance changes dramatically.

In reviewing the statistics I listed in Chapter One, if you are a female who does not have menstrual cycles (i.e., you are a post-menopausal female, a prepubescent female, or you have undergone a hysterectomy), or if you are a male, then the probabilities of your possessing an alkaline, mixed, or acid imbalance are approximately 75%, 12.5%, and 12.5% respectively. If you are a female of the type just described, or if you are a male, then the probability of your possessing a cyclic BioProfile is less than 1%.

Consequently, if you are a female who does not have menstrual cycles, or if you are a male, and you experience "mood swings," or "wellness swings," then it is highly unlikely that these swings may be attributed to a cyclic BioProfile. It is far more likely that these swings *may be attributed to a static metabolic imbalance changing in amplitude or severity as a result of the fact that you have in the past unwittingly been eating foods which are relatively biocompatible, and relatively bio-incompatible.* In other words, in the overwhelming majority of cases, "mood swings" or "wellness swings" are the result of externally or nutritionally driven factors (commonly called *exogenous* factors), and not internally or genetically driven factors (commonly called *endogenous* factors).

If you are a female who has menstrual cycles, then the probabilities of your possessing an alkaline, mixed, or acid imbalance are approximately 60%, 15%, and 15% respectively. If you are a female with active menstrual cycles, then the probability of your possessing a Cyclic BioProfile is approximately 10%. However, if you are a female who has menstrual cycles and well defined cyclic PMS and/or well defined cyclic "mood swings," do *not* jump to the conclusion that you must of necessity possess a Cyclic BioProfile. The statistics suggest instead that most of these swings are probably externally (exogenously) driven and not internally (endogenously) driven.

On the other hand, the probability of your possessing a Cyclic BioProfile is extremely high if your caffeine tolerance changes from positive to negative throughout the course of your menstrual cycle. For example, if you find yourself caffeine-tolerant during one phase of your menstrual cycle but caffeine-intolerant during another phase, then you are almost certainly alkaline during your caffeine-tolerant phase, and nonalkaline (acid or mixed) during your caffeine-intolerant phase.

In fact, as I'll soon discuss in detail, transitions from one metabolic state to another—if and when they occur—almost always occur during certain well-defined key milestones during a woman's menstrual cycle.

It is always important to remember that *individuals possess BioProfiles; disorders do not possess BioProfiles.* Consequently, any attempt to correlate your symptom type with a particular metabolic imbalance will likely prove futile. In plain English, deciphering your BioProfile isn't complicated. Simply gauge your reaction to coffee and take it from there. If you don't know how you react to coffee, or if you've desensitized yourself to caffeine because of caffeine over-consumption, then simply abstain from coffee for 7-10 days and then re-introduce it. The probability is extremely high that after caffeine abstinence for 7-10 days, you will respond to coffee, either positively or negatively.

If you are a woman with menstrual cycles, it's also *critically important* for you to test your caffeine tolerance on *any one typical/ representative day during each* of the three critical phases within your menstrual cycle:

- your menstrual phase: day 28/1 through day 4 in the ideal cycle (non-ideal cycles are discussed below)
- your pre-ovulatory phase: day 4/5 through day 14/15 in the ideal cycle
- your premenstrual phase: day 14/15 through day 28/1 in the ideal cycle

Why? Because *if* you possess a Cyclic BioProfile, and therefore transition from one metabolic state to another, you will in all probability do so at the following times and only at the following times in the ideal cycle:

- when your period begins (day 28/1 in the ideal cycle)
- when your period ends (day 4/5 in the ideal cycle)
- when you ovulate (day 14/15 in the ideal cycle)

Finally, *if your menstrual cycle is not ideal,* then simply apply the caffeine test (or food challenge test - see below) on any one typical or representative day during each of the following phases of your menstrual cycle:

- your menstrual phase (when you are menstruating)
- your pre-ovulatory phase (between the time you stop menstruating and the time you ovulate)
- your premenstrual phase (between the time you ovulate and the time you start menstruating)

Incidentally, *if a woman possesses a Cyclic BioProfile,* then the probability is very high that she transitions through no more than two (of the three possible) static metabolic states. Once again, deciphering your BioProfile should not be made into an unnecessarily complicated state of affairs. It is relatively straightforward. In response to my first book, I received countless letters from women who were convinced that their BioProfiles were characterized by diurnal cycles (over 24 hours) among all three static metabolic states, superimposed onto a 28 day cycle, further superimposed on an annual cycle! It turned out that most of these women did not even possess a Cyclic BioProfile. Their wellness "swings" were completely exogenously driven by the foods they ate. The few women who did possess Cyclic BioProfiles simply transitioned from one metabolic state to another one over a monthly period. These transitions almost invariably occurred at the beginning of one or more of the three menstrual phases listed above. How could their initial assessments have been so far off the mark? Here are some reasons:

- I had not yet discovered the simplicity of the caffeine tolerance test at that time. Other methods were more complex.
- These individuals did not follow my advice nor did they keep accurate food-mood diaries.
- Most people like to believe that they are far more metabolically complex than they really are. Don't fall into this trap.

If you simply cannot drink coffee (say for religious reasons), then you should try and obtain a temporary medical dispensation, or use a high caffeine content, sugar free, soft drink. Alternatively, you may take the food challenge test described below, which excludes coffee, and determine your BioProfile from your reactions to that test. Excluding coffee from the food challenge test will not significantly compromise its reliability in discriminating among the different metabolic types. If you choose the food challenge option, it is critical that you keep a set of accurate food-mood diaries documenting your reactions several times during the day of the test.

As you will note, most of the foods listed in the test are acid inducing. They are meant to neutralize a pre-existing alkaline imbalance, and accentuate a pre-existing nonalkaline imbalance. Consequently, if you are an alkaline metabolizer, the probability is high that you will get at least some symptom relief on the day you take the test. Relief is not necessarily synonymous with complete symptom remission, although complete symptom remission may occur. Conversely, if you are nonalkaline, then you will likely feel worse than usual on your food challenge test day.

WARNING: If you suffer adverse reactions to specific foods and have avoided them in the past, continue to avoid them even though they may be listed as appropriate for your metaboilc type. You may try re-introducing them *(one at a time)* into your regimen after you achieve BioBalance to determine whether your adverse reactions have subsided, as will likely be the case.

CAUTION: DO <u>NOT</u> TAKE THE SUPPLEMENTS APPROPRIATE FOR ALKALINE METABOLIZERS ON YOUR FOOD CHALLENGE TEST DAY.

Why? Because if you happen to be a nonalkaline (acid or mixed) metabolizer, ingesting highly acid-inducing foods in addition to acid-inducing supplements could very well place you in the emergency room! I'm not exaggerating this point. If you don't believe me, you are free, of course, to provoke this type of response. I would suggest that you have a friend act as your patient advocate on the day of your food challenge test if you are crazy enough to try this. However, I strongly recommend that you just take my word for it.

If, from the caffeine tolerance test or food challenge test, you determine that you *are* nonalkaline (acid or mixed), you will subsequently have to try each of the two regimens appropriate for mixed and acid metabolizers to determine which of these two closely related nonalkaline metabolic imbalances you possess. A glance at the nonalkaline case histories that will be reviewed in this book will show you how this may be accomplished in straightforward fashion.

Food Challenge Test

- **BREAKFAST:** 1 cup of coffee with or without 1% fat milk and with or without 1 level teaspoon of sugar - as desired. Coffee may be excluded if prohibited for religious or other reasons, and decaffeinated tea or herbal tea (any variety) may be used instead; half or whole grapefruit with small amount of sugar or honey (sugar or honey optional); 1 or 2 slices of whole grain bread (either Essene or Ezekial bread which may be purchased at any health food store and at many supermarkets).

- **LUNCH:** Vegetarian pasta consisting of any style boiled pasta, stir fried (in very small amount of sesame seed or safflower oil = 1/2-to-1 teaspoon) with broccoli, onions, cabbage, carrots and zucchini (eat slowly and eat as much as you feel you'll need to satisfy your hunger); 1 cup of plain low fat yogurt (1% fat or less) with fresh apple and peach slices. 1 cup of coffee or (if excluded) decaffeinated or herbal tea (any variety).

- **DINNER:** 4-to-6 ounces of poached cod or scrod; boiled brown rice; brussel sprouts; baked squash - any pumpkin-like squash including butternut squash will suffice; (eat slowly and eat as much as you feel you'll need to satisfy your hunger.) 1 cup of any variety of herbal teal (no coffee).

If you dislike this menu plan, then you may make your own from the foods allowed for alkaline metabolizers. Remember not to introduce meats or fish (even of the allowed varieties) until dinner. Your protein source for lunch should be restricted to low fat (1% or less) yogurt. Just be sure not to make your challenge menu too "fancy," and be sure to refrain from adding any significant amount of salt and fat to your foods. You should of course drink water whenever you are thirsty throughout the course of the day.

One final word about coffee. Most of the people I've counseled believed their bad reactions to the food challenge were solely because of the coffee, when in fact they didn't really know why they reacted poorly, because they hadn't had a cup of coffee in years. Why not? Because the health media have generally portrayed coffee as a poisonous drug, and well-meaning, health-conscious people will tend to fault the coffee before they fault their own metabolic imbalance. I can name at least one nationally known holistic physician who refuses to practice BioBalance Therapy because I stated that coffee may have some therapeutic value when correctly administered.

Please remember, I have never said that anyone should live on coffee. Nor have I ever stated that any metabolic type may use coffee. I have stated that coffee has therapeutic value when used correctly, and that the need for coffee among alkaline metabolizers almost always diminishes in a short time once BioBalance is achieved. The moral of this story is, don't waste your time trying to determine how you might react to coffee based on the popular media coverage about coffee. Yes, there are negative effects that can be linked with long-term, heavy, coffee consumption. But I am talking here about a single cup to perform a medical test.

Yes, there are more scientific, more expensive and more time-consuming ways to determine your BioProfile, but your reaction to coffee as a determinant of your BioProfile is inexpensive, accurate and easy to do, and for the vast majority of people, sufficiently accurate to eliminate expensive tests. So simply have a cup of coffee and see how you feel. It's that simple.

If you are alkaline, you might be in for a big surprise. More than a few alkaline metabolizers have reported immediate and significant symptom relief, even remission in some cases within a short time after their first cup. This is especially true of mild to moderate alkaline-induced depression/fatigue. These alkaline metabolizers often wonder why they ever gave up drinking coffee in the first place. In fact, some of these people reported in retrospect that they started a slow process of mental erosion after they got on the health consciousness bandwagon.

If you are one of the very few individuals (less than 1%) who cannot determine your BioProfile based upon the caffeine tolerance test or the food challenge test, then the following brief true/false test may be of assistance.

1. The less I eat, the better I feel. In fact, I've tried fasting in the past and found that I've felt great.
2. After eating meat, fish or poultry for lunch (especially if it is fried as you'd find at a fast food drive-thru or take-out), I find that I get sleepy and/or thirsty later during the day.
3. As far as sex is concerned, I can take it or leave it. Sex doesn't do much for me. Even when it does, it typically takes me a long time to get stimulated.
4. When I go to the dentist I usually don't need Novocain when I have my teeth drilled.

If you've answered true to each of these statements, then you are without a doubt alkaline. In addition to responding well to caffeine, alkaline metabolizers on average respond well to prolonged fasts, poorly to meaty/greasy meals, and typically possess high thresholds to both pleasure and pain. Conversely, if you've answered false to each of these statements then you are almost without a doubt acid/nonalkaline. If you feel like you could answer either true or false to at least 3 out of 4 of these questions, then you are probably a mixed metabolizer.

In any event, the extent to which you are caffeine tolerant should over-ride your responses to this test. In other words, your reaction to coffee should be your primary guide in determining your BioProfile, and you should disregard the above questions if your caffeine tolerance or intolerance is well defined.

Incidentally, as far as fasting is concerned, alkaline metabolizers typically respond well to prolonged (multi-day) fasts. I don't however like to use fasting as the sole criterion for determining an individual's BioProfile for the following two reasons:

1. Many alkaline metabolizers report having a great deal of difficulty during the first and/or second day of their fast even though the overwhelming majority of alkaline metabolizers who manage to get through the first couple of days do quite well thereafter.

2. A significant minority of mixed metabolizers also responds well to fasts (although acid types almost never do).

In other words, fasting is not always as reliable an indicator of your BioProfile as other measures. Also, and perhaps of greater importance, asking most individuals to fast for several days is usually too demanding. If you feel that you can fast for three or four days or more without endangering your health, and find the fast agreeable even though it may be difficult at first, then you are certainly not an acid metabolizer. You are either an alkaline or mixed metabolizer with the odds in your favor of being an alkaline metabolizer.

If you *still* cannot decipher your BioProfile via the caffeine tolerance test, or the food challenge test, or through your responses to the brief questionnaire (above), or via a prolonged fast, then you should simply assume that you are alkaline and adhere to the nutritional regimen appropriate for alkaline metabolizers until you sense a gradual improvement or erosion in your over-all wellness. Why? Because statistics show that the majority of both males and females are alkaline metabolizers. Furthermore, an acid-inducing regimen (appropriate for alkaline metabolizers) seems to provoke both favorable and unfavorable responses *faster* than would be the case if you adhered to either of the nonalkaline-inducing regimens.

Finally, listed below are some questions you should try to answer to test your understanding of BioBalance Therapy in general. See if you can determine each individual-in-question's BioProfile. You need only state whether the person in each case is alkaline or nonalkaline.

1. Clara's physician put her on a high carbohydrate diet to help her lose weight. After being on this diet for about a week, Clara felt hungrier than usual and noticed that she was becoming very short tempered.
2. Sylvia went to her nutritionist to see if she could get help for her inability to fall asleep and remain sleeping. Sylvia's nutritionist prescribed 1500 mgs of calcium (Sylvia's nutritionist euphemistically called the calcium supplements "lull-a-bye pills"), warm whole goat's milk, 1 whole banana, 1000 mgs of inositol and 1000 mgs of choline before bedtime. After taking these supplements and foods for several days, Sylvia found that here sleep problem worsened and that she became very depressed during the early morning hours.
3. Bob is diabetic. He finds that he can reduce his diabetes medication if he (a) adds no fat whatever to his foods and (b) abstains from eating animal foods of all varieties. His only source of protein comes from low fat dairy. He makes up for his reduced dietary intake of B12

(which he would ordinarily get from eating animal foods) by taking 100 mcgs of supplemental B12 daily.

4. Dorothy's physician suggested that she take 800 IUs of vitamin E (mixed tocopherols), 10,000 IUs of vitamin A (palmitate) and increase her daily intake of certain cold water fish for her skin condition. After a week of this treatment Dorothy noted that she was becoming a bit run down. Her physician then went on to recommend that she take weekly B12 shots (1000 mcgs) as "pick-me-ups." Not only did Dorothy not feel "picked up," she actually began to feel worse.

5. Anne noticed that deep fried, meaty fast foods seemed to calm her down when she felt anxious for no apparent reason. Her clinical psychologist from whom she was receiving counseling told Anne that she was seeking solace in food. Specifically, Anne was told that she was feeding her "outer person," when she needed to feed her "inner person," and "inner child." Consequently, Anne was told that she would require more frequent therapy sessions to get "to the root" of her "deep-seated emotional problems," and to examine the *real reason* for her newfound fascination with food.

6. Kathy went to see her doctor about her premenstrual syndrome and chronic fatigue. Her doctor suggested that she take plenty of vitamins B1, B2, and B6 (he called them the "energy vitamins"), and that she eat a high carbohydrate diet. Kathy found substantial improvement from her 1st-through-14th cycle days, but found that her PMS (during days 15 through 28) actually got much worse. Kathy's doctor (a holistic physician specializing in PMS) said that Kathy's problem was likely stress-related, and referred Kathy to a *stress management specialist*.

7. Marty wanted to get the competitive advantage in his golf game. So he went to a sports medicine practitioner who specialized in nutrition. The practitioner told Marty that he should always eat a high carbohydrate snack on the golf course if he felt like he was running down. Marty tried this and found that it helped somewhat.

8. Art's holistic physician told him that he had a partial blockage of an artery. While surgery was not recommended, his physician told him to try eating plenty of legumes and certain cold-water fish such as salmon. Art followed these suggestions faithfully, and noted that he seemed to tire far more easily than he had in the past.

9. Ellen found that by taking lots of B complex vitamins (which disproportionately contained B1, B2, B6 and Niacin), and by eating a high carbohydrate, low fat, diet, she could effectively combat her depression, and stop taking her anti-depressant medications which her psychiatrist had been prescribing, along with intensive psychotherapy, for more than 6 years.

10. Ruth's psychiatrist told her that the only way she was going to lose weight was by "facing up to life, growing up, and becoming a big girl," and by exercising her "will power." Out of desperation, Ruth fasted for almost 10 days, lost 12 pounds and felt more energetic than she had since she was a teenager.

Food Mood Diary

The blank food-mood diary page at the end of this chapter will make it easier to keep your food-mood diary. Make multiple photocopies to track your progress over at least 30 days. If you abide by the guidelines I've provided for you in this book, you'll discover how the food you eat can change the way you feel, and you'll discover a whole new way to achieve and retain higher levels of wellness than you've ever been able to maintain in the past.

The key to your success in BioBalance Therapy is consistency and perseverance. At first you may find that BioBalance is perhaps a bit awkward, especially since you won't be able to eat whatever you want whenever you want it. Anything new always seems awkward at first. I can assure you that after you've mastered the basics of BioBalance Therapy, it will seem quite natural. Indeed you may wonder how you ever managed to live without it.

Most people go through life eating haphazardly. Needless to say, these people randomly drift in and out of sub-optimal levels of psychological and physical well-being. They have no idea why their levels of well-being change as much as they do, and they generally ascribe these fluctuations to factors that are by and large irrelevant. No diet or nutritional regimen and supplements can ward off the stresses we encounter each day throughout our lives. We all have crises and troubles which are external to us, and over which we have little control. However, we can control our internal metabolic environment by appropriate use of BioBalance Therapy. BioBalance Therapy is a very powerful tool that will allow you to control your internal environment by allowing you to achieve and maintain a state of dynamic metabolic equilibrium.

BioBalance will also give you a very significant competitive edge. Remember, BioBalance Therapy really does work. It is not power of suggestion. BioBalance Therapy will dramatically improve your physical and mental well-being. Though you will not be able to escape the stress of life, you will respond to it, not as someone whose energies have already been depleted or exhausted, incapable of dealing with "one more thing," but rather with the inner strength and resources (mental and physical) required of you. Remember, you need not believe in BioBalance Therapy in order for it to work. BioBalance Therapy really does work, but only if you make it work for you.

Sample Food/Mood Diary

NAME:_____ DATE:_____

PHASE OF MENSTRUAL CYCLE:
__ MENSTRUAL   (DAYS 1- 4)
__ PREOVULATORY   (DAYS 5-14)
__ PREMENSTRUAL   (DAYS 15-28)
__ DAY NUMBER IN CYCLE
__ NO CYCLE

Time at Arising:
Sleep Description:
Mood Upon Arising:

Time of Breakfast:
Breakfast:
Mood After Breakfast:

Mood Before Snack:
Midmorning Snack:
Mood After Snack:

Mood Before Lunch:
Time of Lunch:
Lunch:
Mood After Lunch:

Mood Before Snack:
Midafternoon Snack:
Mood After Snack:

Mood Before Dinner:
Time of Dinner:
Dinner:
Mood After Dinner:

Mood Before Retiring:
Time of Retiring:

Chapter

4

Myra L. — An Alkaline Metabolizer:

This chapter introduces you to Myra L, an alkaline metabolizer. She experienced beneficial reactions to her biocompatible nutritional regimen within a matter of days, and suffered adverse side effects within a matter of hours when she strayed from that regimen. The case of Myra L. should give you a good idea of how an alkaline metabolizer can recover from long-standing distress by achieving BioBalance, and then quickly relapse by straying from it. Myra's odyssey into, out of, and then back into BioBalance is summarized through a series of representative food-mood diaries which are included in this chapter.

The first set extends from July 11th to July 18th, and illustrates Myra's reaction to the first phase of BioBalance Therapy, *not* including supplementation with vitamins and minerals. Let me re-emphasize that *all* individuals, irrespective of their BioProfiles, should fine-tune their nutritional regimen(s) *over a minimum 30 day time period prior to introducing their biocompatible supplements.* This is especially true of non-alkaline metabolizers since they will have to determine whether they are acid or mixed mode. The next two chapters will show you how this is accomplished. The second set of diaries (below) illustrates Myra's reaction to the second phase of BioBalance Therapy which *does* include supplementation with biocompatible vitamins and minerals.

After reading my first book, Myra initially determined that she was a static alkaline metabolizer. Note in the diaries that follow, that Myra's caffeine tolerance decreased after she achieved BioBalance during phase two of her therapy as she began taking supplements. This phenomenon is common among alkaline metabolizers. She found that she could no longer tolerate caffeine as well as she did initially. Consequently, she ultimately found that she required only small amounts of caffeine on relatively infrequent occasions to pull herself out of an alkaline slump.

As explained in Chapter One, she did not make any substantial modifications in her nutritional regimen after she achieved BioBalance. Once again, (absent some fine-tuning) the nutritional regimen required by any static metabolic type required to *maintain* BioBalance is the same regimen required to *achieve* BioBalance. You can see in Myra's case that her inadvertent and temporary switch on July 16th (lunch and dinner) to a regimen appropriate for mixed metabolizers after she achieved BioBalance resulted in a return of her pre-BioBalance symptoms within a matter of hours.

Myra is 55 years old and initially complained of chronic fatigue, insomnia, depression, body aches and pains especially in her lower back, neck and shoulder blade area, and bloating in her abdomen accompanied by gas and alternate bouts of constipation and diarrhea. She also stated that she was approximately 15 to 20 pounds overweight, and that as hard as she might try, she found it impossible to lose weight. Myra had tried a number of different therapies, both nutritional and otherwise, all to no avail. She had discovered BioBalance Therapy through a friend who had read my first book, **BioBalance: How to Use Acid/Alkaline Nutrition to Solve the Food-Mood-Health Puzzle,** and had benefited from it. Myra decided to follow the book's guidelines. She adhered strictly to the nutritional recommendations appropriate for static alkaline metabolizers listed in that book's appendix. Her response was favorable and rapid until she started "cheating" or straying from the nutritional regimen appropriate for her. Overall, she managed to dispel her symptoms within several days, and almost effortlessly achieved her ideal weight in less than three months. Incidentally, this was the first time Myra had achieved her ideal weight in more than eight years.

The nutritional regimen, which caused Myra's mental and physical performance to peak, is the one listed in this book's appendix under the heading, "Nutritional Regimen Appropriate for Alkaline Metabolizers." I would encourage you to carefully review this regimen whether or not you are an alkaline metabolizer. Myra's nutritional regimen is to a large extent the mirror image opposite of the nutritional regimen appropriate for acid metabolizers, and the near mirror image opposite of the nutritional regimen appropriate for mixed metabolizers. By familiarizing yourself with Myra's regimen, you'll get a good idea of how foods should be universally categorized regardless of your BioProfile.

Myra's nutritional regimen was the basic original model regimen appropriate for all alkaline metabolizers found in my first book. The improved and reformulated version of the nutritional regimen appropriate for alkaline metabolizers, is, in fact, the macrobiotic diet, discussed in Chapters One and Two. Incidentally, upon follow-up contact, Myra chose to shift over to macrobiotics, and found that she felt even better. Specifically, macrobiotics helped her eliminate some occasional nuisance problems that were likely caused by lactose intolerance. (Myra's diaries reflecting her switch to macrobiotics are not listed below.)

In any event, all alkaline metabolizers should adhere to a nutritional regimen characterized by low fat, low sodium (salt), and low purine cuisine. Myra was careful to use salt, oil and fats of any variety very sparingly. She also never ate meat, fish or poultry *of any variety* (even the allowed varieties) before midafternoon. Myra discovered that she did best by eating light cuisine throughout the entire day, avoiding meat, fish or poultry, even of the allowed varieties, until dinner. At times, Myra did especially well by abstaining from meat, fish and poultry (of the allowed varieties) for the course of the entire day.

You may think that the description I've provided for you of Myra's diet is simply "common sense" based upon what the popular press and the experts are telling you. Consequently, you may feel it is unnecessary to read the detailed version of Myra's diet in the appendix at the end of this book. Please do not to make that mistake. I would be doing you a disservice if I provided you with nothing more than an overview of Myra's diet. Her nutritional regimen, as is the case for all alkaline metabolizers, goes far beyond what is currently touted as "sensible eating" within both popular and professional circles. It is a serious mistake to think that "eating light" or "sensibly," as defined by the popular media, will suffice for an alkaline metabolizer such as Myra. In the preceding paragraph I said that eating light cuisine is necessary if and only if you are an alkaline type. However, simply eating light fare is not enough if you are alkaline like Myra. As explained in Chapter One it is important for alkaline metabolizers to restrict their intake of certain proteins called nucleoproteins or purines.

This is one basis of the nutritional regimen appropriate for alkaline metabolizers. Once again, simply "eating light" is not enough if you are doing so with disregard to nucleoprotein or purine intake. That's why a careful review of the dietary regimen in the appendix is so important.

I keep hammering away at this point because of many discouraging letters I received from alkaline metabolizers who read my first book. Specifically, these particular readers made it clear that they simply adhered to what they thought was "a light diet" without studying the details of the regimen appropriate for alkaline metabolizers recommended by BioBalance Therapy. Sadly, far too many people are looking for instantaneous enlightenment, magic bullets and quick fixes, through clever sound bytes, and have little interest in taking the time to read, study and apply. BioBalance Therapy probably won't help you if you fall into that category.

There are many foods which the nutritional and medical communities might endorse as being "wholesome" and "sensible" and which fall into the category of light fare or light cuisine, but which are ill-suited to Myra and alkaline types like her. These foods are listed in the appendix at the end of this book. Even though I listed many of these foods in Chapter One, let me give you a few examples by way of review.

Legumes are highly alkaline inducing. They are, therefore, inappropriate for Myra. Eating legumes (peas, beans, lentils and peanuts) is the mistake most commonly made by alkaline types during recovery. This error is understandable since legumes are low in fat, and since the popular/professional press routinely tells us how good these foods are for our health. There are some people who will indeed benefit from these foods, but Myra isn't one of them, and you're not either if you're an alkaline metabolizer. Remember, as explained in Chapter Two, that alkaline metabolizers *must* eat legumes in small-to-moderate quantities *if and only if* they adhere to the improved reformulation of the nutritional regimen appropriate for alkaline metabolizers, namely the macrobiotic regimen.

If you are an alkaline metabolizer and decide not to adhere to a macrobiotic regimen, then you should eat legumes sparingly, and ideally try to avoid them altogether.

If you look at Myra's food-mood diary for July 16th, you'll see that her lunch appears to be acceptable to an individual unfamiliar with BioBalance Therapy. It is light and devoid of animal protein. Notably,

Myra tells us that it is also "all-natural." The fact that foods may be "all-natural" is of little significance if those foods are inappropriate for your metabolic type. After studying the appendix, you'll see that the legumes (beans) in her vegetarian chili as well as the spinach, artichoke hearts, asparagus tips, garbanzo beans and mushrooms in Myra's salad were completely inappropriate for her metabolic type.

Given the fact that Myra tended to metabolize in an alkaline mode, and given the fact that these foods tended to make Myra more alkaline than she was normally, these foods spelled disaster for her.

Look at the reaction she reports for proof of the fact that she strayed nutritionally. While her adverse reaction was not instantaneous, it did occur over a period of several hours after she ate in a fashion completely inappropriate for her metabolic type. Many of Myra's old symptoms for which she originally sought treatment returned quickly. Notably, these symptoms had vanished within a few days after Myra had embarked upon her program of BioBalance Therapy. Similarly, Myra's dinner on July 16th was also inappropriate for her. Salmon, string beans and cauliflower are also highly alkaline-inducing, and so accentuated Myra's underlying alkaline metabolic imbalance. Myra's dinner served to compound the ill effects of her lunch and produced additional ill effects which maintained a grip on her through the night. After resuming her therapeutic regimen on the following day, it took Myra the better part of 24 hours to regain her previous and new-found sense of well-being.

A few additional remarks about Myra's nutritional regimen deserve attention. You may be shocked that Myra's regimen includes coffee, indeed strong black coffee with sugar for breakfast, and at times, later in the day. You may feel that coffee is a drug, and as a drug it should be avoided. Well, you're partly correct. Coffee is indeed a drug, but so is brown rice, broccoli, fillet of sole and orange juice. The idea in BioBalance Therapy is to adhere to a nutritional regimen that will countereffect your underlying biochemical or metabolic imbalance and thereby allow you to achieve a state of BioBalance leading to optimal physical/mental well-being. Frequent and long-term ingestion of coffee and sugar is a health hazard. Coffee does, however, have short-term therapeutic value when ingested by alkaline types in controlled moderation.

I've observed over the years that an alkaline metabolizer such as Myra will require less coffee to maintain BioBalance once she achieves it. Several weeks after achieving BioBalance, Myra found that she didn't need any more than one cup of coffee daily, and oftentimes could function very well without any coffee at all. This was especially true after Myra began taking the vitamin/mineral supplements appropriate for her metabolic type. These supplements are also detailed in the appendix. I have included two days of food-mood diaries which Myra completed after she began taking her supplements. These diaries were completed on August 21st and August 22nd.

You'll note that Myra initially reported a mild flush reaction (similar to a mild sunburn) to the niacin in her supplements. This reaction is common and normal. This reaction usually disappears within an hour, may recur on occasion in the future after this supplement is taken again, and typically does not cause any discomfort. In the unlikely event it had caused any discomfort, Myra would have cut her daily dose of niacin in half. Myra was observant and realized that her vitamin/mineral supplements accentuated the acid induction potential of her foods, and eventually she no longer needed to rely upon extremely acid inducing foods such as coffee to countereffect her alkaline imbalance and maintain a state of BioBalance. In fact, her reaction on the afternoon of August 21st reveals that she pushed her metabolism a bit too hard in drinking a midafternoon cup of coffee after eating a light lunch *and* taking her supplements as well. While Myra's response to coffee in the past was almost invariably favorable, after achieving BioBalance Myra responded to coffee by becoming somewhat tense, nervous and slightly nauseous. Myra realized her error, fine-tuned her diet by further limiting her intake of coffee and did not repeat this mistake again.

Finally, I should emphasize that *vitamin/mineral supplements should not be used as a license to cheat.* I've seen some people rationalize cheating nutritionally by stating that their supplements will offset any of their foods' bad effects. If you take supplements appropriate for your BioProfile but eat haphazardly, you are deluding yourself. You won't feel any better, and you may as well save your money by not taking any supplements at all. It's been my experience that dietary nutrition, without any supplements, is responsible for at least 75% and as much as 90% of an individual's recovery. Some people simply cannot tolerate supplements of any variety. That's precisely why I repeatedly state that you should first determine your BioProfile through nutrition alone, and then introduce your BioProfile-compatible vitamin/mineral supplements. If you find that for any reason you cannot take these supplements then DON'T TAKE THEM! This handicap is relatively minor. If you can't take supplements you should by no means give up BioBalance Therapy since it is highly likely that you will still derive very substantial benefits from the nutritional regimen appropriate for you.

Myra's Food/Mood Diary — Day 1
(no supplements involved)

NAME: Myra, L. DATE: July 11, 2000
PHASE OF MENSTRUAL CYCLE:
__ MENSTRUAL (DAYS 1- 4)
__ PREOVULATORY (DAYS 5-14)
__ PREMENSTRUAL (DAYS 15-28)
X NO CYCLE

Time at Arising: 7 am
Sleep Description: 9 hours – broken sleep, very poor.
Mood Upon Arising: very tired and depressed, body aches stiffness, joints ache.

Time of Breakfast: 8:00 am
Breakfast: strong black coffee with 1 teaspoon of sugar, glass of orange juice, slice of plain whole grain bread.
Mood After Breakfast: somewhat better, stiffness and aching decreased, spirits lifted a bit

---

Mood Before Snack: getting tired around 10:30 a.m., a bit stiff
Midmorning Snack: 1 tangerine and 1 cup of coffee (no sugar)

Mood After Snack: refreshed, somewhat more motivated

Mood Before Lunch: getting tired again, would like to
   nap, lower back and shoulder blades hurt
Time of Lunch: 12:30 pm
Lunch: 4 ounces of skim yogurt with fruit –
   tangerine slices, grapefruit, pineapple, grapes
   and melon, herbal tea.
Mood After Lunch: a little gassy, but otherwise ok,
   energized

Mood Before Snack: yawning a lot, would like to
   nap again
Midafternoon Snack: I tangerine and I cup of
   coffee (no sugar)
Mood After Snack: energized (had bowel movement –
   felt much better, gassiness gone)

Mood Before Dinner: ok
Time of Dinner: 7:00 pm
Dinner: 4 ounces of broiled fillet of flounder, brown
   rice and broccoli, lemon, herbal tea.
Mood After Dinner: relaxed, more energy than usual
   for this time of day

Mood Before Retiring: very tired
Time of Retiring: 11:00 pm

Myra's Food/Mood Diary — Day 2

NAME: *Myra, L.*　　　　　　DATE: *July 12, 2000*
PHASE OF MENSTRUAL CYCLE:
__　MENSTRUAL　　　　　(DAYS 1- 4)
__　PREOVULATORY　　　　(DAYS 5-14)
__　PREMENSTRUAL　　　　(DAYS 15-28)
X　NO CYCLE

Time at Arising: *6:30 am*
Sleep Description: *7 1/2 hours broken, awakened*
　often to urinate.
Mood Upon Arising: *poor, tired, depressed, body aching*

Time of Breakfast: *7:15 am*
Breakfast: *strong black coffee with sugar, whole*
　grain bread, 1/2 grapefruit
Mood After Breakfast: *more energy, cheerful, body*
　aches have diminished

Mood Before Snack: *getting tired again*
Midmorning Snack: *coffee with sugar, 1 tangerine,*
　8 ounces of water
Mood After Snack: *better*

Mood Before Lunch: *ok*
Time of Lunch: *11:45 am*
Lunch: *salad with tomatoes, lettuce, cucumbers,*
　shredded raw cabbage, onions, low fat mozzarella
　cheese, 1 tsp. olive oil and squeezed lemon, herbal
　tea with lemon.
Mood After Lunch: *energized*

Mood Before Snack: sleepy, want to take a nap
Midafternoon Snack: 2 raw sweet peppers and 1 rice
    cake, coffee, 8 ounces of water
Mood After Snack: much better, motivated

Mood Before Dinner: tired again
Time of Dinner: 6:00 pm
Dinner: 2 egg omelet with onion, pepper and
    tomato, low salt tomato sauce, brown rice,
    steamed cabbage, herbal tea (no sugar)
Mood After Dinner: better, less tired

Mood Before Retiring: tired (normal for this hour)
Time of Retiring: 11:30 pm

Myra's Food/Mood Diary — Day 3

NAME: Myra, L.   DATE: July 13, 2000
PHASE OF MENSTRUAL CYCLE:
__ MENSTRUAL   (DAYS 1- 4)
__ PREOVULATORY   (DAYS 5-14)
__ PREMENSTRUAL   (DAYS 15-28)
X NO CYCLE

Time at Arising: 7:00 am
Sleep Description: 7 1/2 hours, better than usual
Mood Upon Arising: so-so, no significant body aches

Time of Breakfast: 7:30 am
Breakfast: strong black coffee with sugar, 2 ounces
    low fat yogurt, 1/2 grapefruit.
Mood After Breakfast: better, energized and motivated

Mood Before Snack: a little tired but not too bad
Midmorning Snack: rice cake and raw sweet pepper,

8 ounces of water
Mood After Snack: *better*

Mood Before Lunch: *good*
Time of Lunch: *12:00 pm*
Lunch: *low fat (1%) yogurt with fruit: strawberries, blueberries, pineapple, apple, grapes, herbal tea with lemon (no sugar).*
Mood After Lunch: *good*

Mood Before Snack: *running down, getting tired*
Midafternoon Snack: *coffee, tangerine and rice cake, 8 ounces of water*
Mood After Snack: *much better*

Mood Before Dinner: *ok*
Time of Dinner: *6:30 pm*
Dinner: *chicken breast fillet, pasta with low fat, low salt tomato sauce, salad with tomatoes, sweet peppers, onions, cabbage, carrot slivers, 3 olives (well rinsed to get rid of salt) with squeezed lemon and 1 teaspoon of safflower oil, herbal tea.*
Mood After Dinner: *good*

Mood Before Retiring: *still good*
Time of Retiring: *10:30 pm*

Myra's Food/Mood Diary — Day 4

NAME: Myra, L.   DATE: July 14, 2000
PHASE OF MENSTRUAL CYCLE:
__ MENSTRUAL   (DAYS 1- 4)
__ PREOVULATORY   (DAYS 5-14)
__ PREMENSTRUAL   (DAYS 15-28)
X   NO CYCLE

Time at Arising: 7:00 am
Sleep Description: 8 hours, best sleep I've had
    in a long time
Mood Upon Arising: calm, relaxed, ready to get going

Time of Breakfast: 7:30 am
Breakfast: strong black coffee,
    1 rice cake, 1/2 apple.
Mood After Breakfast: cheerful, upbeat, energetic

Mood Before Snack: ok
Midmorning Snack: 1 tangerine, 1 rice cake, herbal tea
Mood After Snack: GREAT! euphoric, energetic,
    very upbeat.

Mood Before Lunch: still going strong
Time of Lunch: 1:00 pm
Lunch: microwaved left-over flounder fillet (2 ounces),
    1/2 baked potato, 1/2 cooked zucchini, herbal tea
    with lemon.
Mood After Lunch: good

Mood Before Snack: a little tired
Midafternoon Snack: 1/2 grapefruit, 8 ounces of water
Mood After Snack: energized

Mood Before Dinner: still good
Time of Dinner: 6:30 pm
Dinner: baked scrod with lemon, steamed
    broccoli, 1/2 baked acorn squash, whole millet,
    herbal tea with lemon.
Mood After Dinner: good

Mood Before Retiring: relaxed, sleepy
Time of Retiring: 10:00 pm

Myra's Food/Mood Diary — Day 5

NAME: Myra, L.   DATE: July 15, 2000
PHASE OF MENSTRUAL CYCLE:
__ MENSTRUAL   (DAYS 1- 4)
__ PREOVULATORY   (DAYS 5-14)
__ PREMENSTRUAL   (DAYS 15-28)
X NO CYCLE

Time at Arising: 6:00 am
Sleep Description: 8 hours, slept soundly
Mood Upon Arising: relaxed, awake, alert

Time of Breakfast: 6:30 am
Breakfast: strong black coffee, 1 tangerine, 1 rice cake.
Mood After Breakfast: good

Mood Before Snack: still good
Midmorning Snack: not hungry - none, 8 ounces of water
Mood After Snack: still good

Mood Before Lunch: even-tempered, motivated
Time of Lunch: 1:00 pm

Lunch: *pasta salad with noodles, shredded cabbage, cherry tomatoes, diced peppers, chives and low fat yogurt (no mayonnaise), 1 glass orange juice, herbal tea with lemon.*
Mood After Lunch: *good, ready to resume work*

Mood Before Snack: *good*
Midafternoon Snack: *not hungry - none, 8 ounces of water*
Mood After Snack: *still good*

Mood Before Dinner: *good*
Time of Dinner: *6:00 pm*
Dinner:*vegetarian rice pilaf - boiled brown rice baked with tomatoes, small amount low fat, low salt mozzarella cheese, zucchini, sliced hard boiled egg,   roasted peppers, onions; herbal tea with lemon.*
Mood After Dinner: *good, energetic*

Mood Before Retiring: *relaxed, sleepy*
Time of Retiring: *10:30 pm*

Myra's Food/Mood Diary — Day 6

NAME: *Myra, L.*   DATE: *July 16, 2000*
PHASE OF MENSTRUAL CYCLE:
__ MENSTRUAL   (DAYS 1- 4)
__ PREOVULATORY   (DAYS 5-14)
__ PREMENSTRUAL   (DAYS 15-28)
X NO CYCLE

Time at Arising: *6:30 am*
Sleep Description: *8 hours, ·slept very well*

Mood Upon Arising: refreshed and calm, no body aches or stiffness!

Time of Breakfast: 7:00 am
Breakfast: strong black coffee, 1/2 grapefruit, 1 rice cake.
Mood After Breakfast: good

Mood Before Snack: still good
Midmorning Snack: not hungry - none, 8 ounces of water
Mood After Snack: still good

Mood Before Lunch: good
Time of Lunch: 12:30 pm
Lunch: bowl of "all-natural" vegetarian chili with lots of red beans, plus spinach salad with garbanzo beans, artichoke hearts, asparagus tips and mushrooms and olive oil dressing, herbal tea.
Mood After Lunch: good

Mood Before Snack: not so good, tired and very thirsty
Midafternoon Snack: none, 12 ounces of water
Mood After Snack: tired and irritable, want to take a nap

Mood Before Dinner: exhausted
Time of Dinner: 8:00 pm
Dinner: (ate out) cream of cauliflower soup, broiled salmon steak, sauteed string beans and almonds, buttered baked potato with whole sour cream and chives; tea
Mood After Dinner: exhausted, headache, thirsty, want to sleep

---

Mood Before Retiring: same - awful, bad headache
Time of Retiring: 9:00 pm

Myra's Food/Mood Diary — Day 7

NAME: Myra, L.   DATE: July 17, 2000
PHASE OF MENSTRUAL CYCLE:
__ MENSTRUAL   (DAYS 1- 4)
__ PREOVULATORY   (DAYS 5-14)
__ PREMENSTRUAL   (DAYS 15-28)
X NO CYCLE

Time at Arising: 8:30 am
Sleep Description: 11 1/2 hours, poor, tossed and
    turned all night
Mood Upon Arising: awful, depressed,
    swollen joints, cried.

Time of Breakfast: 9:30 am
Breakfast: strong black coffee with sugar,
    12 ounces of water.
Mood After Breakfast: still lousy, very crabby, bloated

Mood Before Snack: same
Midmorning Snack: strong black coffee with sugar,
    8 ounces of water
Mood After Snack: better (bowel movement),
    body not as stiff

Mood Before Lunch: just barely ok
Time of Lunch: 1:00 pm
Lunch: fresh fruit salad: strawberries, grapes, melon,
    grapefruit, pineapple, apple slices, herbal tea.
Mood After Lunch: somewhat better

Mood Before Snack: *getting tired*
Midafternoon Snack: *tangerine, black coffee*
Mood After Snack: *better*

Mood Before Dinner: *ok*
Time of Dinner: *6:00 pm*
Dinner: *boiled brown rice, steamed cabbage, water
    (don't feel like eating very much)*
Mood After Dinner: *ok*

Mood Before Retiring: *better than all day, pretty tired*
Time of Retiring: *8:00 pm*

Myra's Food/Mood Diary — Day 8

NAME: *Myra, L.*   DATE: *July 18, 2000*
PHASE OF MENSTRUAL CYCLE:
__ MENSTRUAL   (DAYS 1- 4)
__ PREOVULATORY   (DAYS 5-14)
__ PREMENSTRUAL   (DAYS 15-28)
X   NO CYCLE

Time at Arising: *5:30 am*
Sleep Description: *9 1/2 hours, pretty well*
Mood Upon Arising: *ok, no major complaints,
    no body aches*

Time of Breakfast: *6:00 am*
Breakfast: *strong black coffee, 8 ounces of water*
Mood After Breakfast: *energized, cheerful (big
    difference over yesterday!)*

Mood Before Snack: *good*
Midmorning Snack: *grapefruit sections, herbal tea
    with honey and lemon*

79

Mood After Snack: good

Mood Before Lunch: good
Time of Lunch: 12:30 pm
Lunch: salad: lettuce, cucumbers, low fat yogurt,
    scallions, cabbage, raisins, apples, herbal tea
Mood After Lunch: energized

Mood Before Snack: still good
Midafternoon Snack: tangerine, coffee, 8 ounces of
    water
Mood After Snack: cheerful and energetic

Mood Before Dinner: same
Time of Dinner: 7:00 pm
Dinner: baked scrod, mustard greens, rice cakes,
    spaghetti squash, herbal tea
Mood After Dinner: feeling very well

Mood Before Retiring: sleepy
Time of Retiring: 10:00 PM

Myra's Food/Mood Diaries
(*With Supplements*)

Note: Myra tested her nutritional regimen for approximately one month without supplements before introducing the vitamins and minerals appropriate for her metabolic type. Myra took a full dose of supplements (see appendix) after breakfast, and another full dose after lunch.

Myra's Food/Mood Diary — Day 1

NAME: Myra, L.   DATE: August 21, 2000
PHASE OF MENSTRUAL CYCLE:
__ MENSTRUAL   (DAYS 1- 4)
__ PREOVULATORY   (DAYS 5-14)
__ PREMENSTRUAL   (DAYS 15-28)
X NO CYCLE

Time at Arising: 6:30 am
Sleep Description: 8 hours, excellent
Mood Upon Arising: calm, refreshed and relaxed

Time of Breakfast: 7:00 am (starting supplements today - will take them only after breakfast and lunch)
Breakfast: herbal tea with lemon, 2 ounces of skim yogurt, 1 tangerine.
Mood After Breakfast: energy high, very motivated, well focused, slight flush reaction to niacin, no big deal

---

Mood Before Snack: great
Midmorning Snack: none, not hungry, 8 ounces of water
Mood After Snack: great

Mood Before Lunch: still up

Time of Lunch: 1:00 pm
Lunch: *fish fillet sandwich, baked scrod on whole rye bread with tomato and lettuce, 1 apple, herbal tea with lemon.*
Mood After Lunch: *cheerful, energetic, motivated (mild flush)*

Mood Before Snack: *same*
Midafternoon Snack: *1 cup of all-natural water processed coffee with brown sugar*
Mood After Snack: *a little tense and anxious, slightly nauseous – can't drink too much coffee and take these supplements at the same time.*

Mood Before Dinner: *somewhat better, getting hungry*
Time of Dinner: 6:00 pm
Dinner: *chicken breast fillet, steamed buckwheat groats with 1/2 teaspoon of olive oil, broccoli and summer squash.*
Mood After Dinner: *good*

Mood Before Retiring: *still good*
Time of Retiring: 11:00 pm

Myra's Food/Mood Diary — Day 2

NAME: *Myra, L.*   DATE: *August 22, 2000*
PHASE OF MENSTRUAL CYCLE:
__ MENSTRUAL   (DAYS 1- 4)
__ PREOVULATORY   (DAYS 5-14)
__ PREMENSTRUAL   (DAYS 15-28)
X NO CYCLE

Time at Arising: *6:30 am*
Sleep Description: *7 1/2 hours deep sleep*

Mood Upon Arising: *fine as usual*

Time of Breakfast: *7:00 am*
Breakfast: *1 glass of orange/grapefruit mix,*
   1 cup of cooked whole oats with
   1% fat milk, 1 rice cake.
Mood After Breakfast: *calm, cheerful, motivated*

Mood Before Snack: *same*
Midmorning Snack: *1 apple, herbal tea,*
   8 ounces of water
Mood After Snack: *same*

Mood Before Lunch: *very slightly tired but not too bad*
Time of Lunch: *12:30 pm*
Lunch: *home made vegetable soup (brown rice,*
   onions, potatoes, leeks, cabbage, broccoli and
   tomatoes in water base), 2 ounces of fillet of
   sole, herbal tea with lemon.
Mood After Lunch: *energized, well focused*

Mood Before Snack: *same*
Midafternoon Snack: *none*
Mood After Snack: *same*

Mood Before Dinner: *same*
Time of Dinner: *7:00 pm*
Dinner: *chicken salad with chicken breast, celery,*
   onions, lettuce, red radishes and dressing of
   skim yogurt + very small amount of mayonnaise,
   white rice,   herbal tea with lemon.
Mood After Dinner: *feel fine*

Mood Before Retiring: *good*
Time of Retiring: *10:30 pm*

Before ending this chapter, I'd like to give you a sample menu consisting of foods appropriate for alkaline metabolizers. The seven-day menu listed below should give you a specific idea as to how alkaline metabolizers must eat if they are to achieve and maintain a state of BioBalance. You may of course create your own menu provided you do so within the nutritional guidelines I've provided for you in the appendix. I don't list snacks for alkaline metabolizers because I've observed that most alkaline metabolizers who snack do so to satisfy mouth hunger and are doing themselves a metabolic disservice. If an alkaline metabolizer must snack, a piece of allowed fruit (any fruit except for bananas or avocados) is permitted.

It is also very important that alkaline metabolizers keep well hydrated (drink plenty of water). This is especially true in the early part of BioBalance Therapy when they may be drinking more than one cup of coffee each day. Coffee, while very acid-inducing, is also a diuretic and will result in water loss. So drinking water on a regular basis is very important for alkaline metabolizers, especially during hot weather. You'll note that I repeatedly list herbal tea as a beverage of choice. Don't feel constrained to use herbal tea or regular tea. Water may be substituted for tea at any time.

Many alkaline metabolizers report that the diet appropriate for them is "no fun," since no gravies or sauces are allowed. While the objective of BioBalance Therapy does not include giving you new "taste sensations," I can understand the need for some variety. Consequently, I've devised some sauces which you may find appealing. These sauces are of course not allowed if you are an alkaline metabolizer and decide to adhere to macrobiotics, the ideal regimen appropriate for alkaline metabolizers.

Tomato sauce may be prepared with fresh or canned tomatoes (low salt or well rinsed), a small amount of safflower oil, fresh garlic, fresh parsley, bay leaves, and any other herbs which you may want to add. This mixture should be brought to a full boil and then allowed to simmer for several hours until thick, or until its consistency is to your liking. You may add this sauce to pasta or rice. You may also add the following ingredients to this sauce if you desire: white meat chicken (breast meat), or allowed fish ("marinara" style). I would suggest that you cook the sauce first, and that the fish or poultry be cooked separately and added later. I must emphasize that this book is not a cookbook, so you're going to have to experiment to determine what cooking process is right for you. To save yourself time and to avoid unnecessary tedium, you may also want to cook a large amount of sauce, store it in your refrigerator or freezer and use it to prepare several meals.

White sauce (or low fat, low salt "Alfredo Sauce") may be prepared with skim or 1% milk and flour. Potato flour or starch will add consistency. Melt 1 tablespoon of low salt margarine (not butter) over low heat. Off heat, blend in 1 tablespoon of flour until smooth. Gradually add 1 cup of low fat or skim milk stirring continuously. Let simmer for 2 to 3 minutes. [Note: 1 tablespoon is equivalent to 3 teaspoons. This is the amount of margarine used in the recipe, and it is far too much fat for an alkaline type to eat at one meal. Consequently, you should use this sauce sparingly, making sure that you don't consume more than 1/3 to 1/2 of the amount listed in this recipe at any one meal.] Once again, you'll have to experiment with this combination to achieve the consistency you most prefer. Cooking a large quantity of this sauce and refrigerating it will allow you to use it on several occasions.

Sample One Week Menu Appropriate for Alkaline Types

Here's a sample of how an alkaline type might eat during a seven-day period. Once again, this sample does not reflect the premier reformulation of the regimen appropriate for alkaline metabolizers, namely macrobiotics (found in Chapter Two), which is the regimen I would recommend.

Day 1
Breakfast: Coffee with 1 level teaspoon of sugar, 1/2 grapefruit, 1 cup of cooked oats with skim milk.

Lunch: Salad: lettuce, cherry tomatoes, shredded cabbage, cucumbers, onions, sliced hard boiled egg; dressing to consist of small amount of olive oil, minced garlic and fresh squeezed lemon; herbal tea (any variety) with squeezed lemon.

Dinner: Flounder fillet, summer squash, boiled potatoes; herbal tea (any variety) with squeezed lemon.

Day 2

Breakfast: Coffee, orange juice, cream of rice with skim milk

Lunch: Chicken salad sandwich with white meat (chicken breast) and lettuce; dressing to consist of low fat yogurt (0% or 1% fat), small amount of mayonnaise, chopped pepper and onion; herbal tea (any variety) with squeezed lemon.

Dinner: Baked scrod, brown rice, steamed broccoli, herbal tea (any variety) with squeezed lemon.

Day 3

Breakfast: Coffee, low fat (skim or 1%) yogurt with raw oats and mixed fruits (any variety except avocados and bananas) such as: apple slices, raisins, pineapple chunks, berries, cherries, melons and grapes.

Lunch: Tuna and potato salad: well-rinsed water-packed fancy white albacore tuna (not chunk light, especially if packed in oil), boiled potatoes, chopped onions, peppers, and lettuce; small amount of olive oil, pressed garlic and fresh squeezed lemon; herbal tea (any variety) with squeezed lemon.

Dinner: Stuffed bell peppers stuffed with brown rice, red sauce (see above) with diced pieces of any of the allowed meats, fish or poultry; salad with lettuce, peppers, tomatoes, onions with small amount of olive oil, garlic and squeezed lemon; herbal tea (any variety) with squeezed lemon.

Day 4

Breakfast: Coffee, grapefruit juice, sugar-free corn flakes with skim milk.

Lunch: Low fat cottage cheese (1% or skim) with any combination of mixed fruit (except banana or avocado); herbal tea (any variety) with squeezed lemon.

Dinner: Fettucini (or any pasta) and chicken breast with low fat/low salt Alfredo/white sauce (see earlier recipe), with stir fried vegetables (in very small amount of olive oil) - vegetables may include onions, zucchini, eggplant and sweet (i.e. bell) peppers; herbal tea (any variety) with squeezed lemon.

Day 5

Breakfast: Coffee, apple juice, bran muffin with jam - any variety (jam optional - preferably sugar free)

Lunch: Well-rinsed fancy white meat albacore tuna salad sandwich with lettuce; dressing to consist of low fat yogurt (skim or 1% fat) and small amount of mayonnaise; herbal tea (any variety) with squeezed lemon.

Dinner: Omelet (2 eggs cooked on Teflon - no added fat) with minced onions, peppers and tomatoes, brown rice, steamed cabbage and onions with no salt, spicy seasonings such as dried red peppers or herb salt substitute (if desired); herbal tea (any variety) with squeezed lemon.

Day 6

Breakfast: Coffee, orange juice, cream of wheat with skim milk

Lunch: Low fat yogurt (skim or 1%) with mixed fruit (any variety except avocados and bananas); herbal tea (any variety) with squeezed lemon.

Dinner: Pasta (any variety) with marinara sauce (see above) - seafood in marinara sauce may contain scrod; steamed broccoli; herbal tea (any variety) with squeezed lemon.

Day 7

Breakfast: Coffee, mixed fruits (except for bananas and avocados); pancake(s) (cooked in Teflon - no added fat) with small amount of real maple syrup

Lunch: Salad containing lettuce, cherry tomatoes, shredded cabbage, cucumbers, onions, sliced hard boiled egg; dressing to consist of small amount of olive oil, minced garlic and fresh squeezed lemon; herbal tea (any variety) with squeezed lemon.

Dinner: Chicken breast baked or broiled and brown rice seasoned with low fat/low salt Alfredo/white sauce, zucchini, herbal tea (any variety) with squeezed lemon

Remember, if you're an alkaline metabolizer, you won't want to overeat since overeating is almost as detrimental to your well-being as eating foods that are incompatible with your BioProfile.

Chapter
5

Gloria R. — An Acid Metabolizer:

In this chapter you'll meet Gloria R, an acid metabolizer. Metabolically, Gloria is the mirror image opposite of Myra whose case history was reviewed in Chapter Four. If you reviewed the portion of the appendix detailing the nutritional regimen appropriate for alkaline metabolizers, you already know something about how Gloria should eat. Specifically, she should eat whatever is off limits to alkaline metabolizers, and conversely she should not eat those foods that form the basis of Myra's regimen.

As far as supplemental vitamins and minerals are concerned, Gloria should take the supplements that are not included in the list of supplements appropriate for Myra. Vitamin C is the only exception. If you read the appendix entitled "Nutritional Regimen Appropriate for Acid Metabolizers," you'll understand precisely why this is so.

I should mention that the nutritional regimen appropriate for acid metabolizers has generated considerable criticism within conventional nutritional and medical circles. You will note that this alkaline-inducing regimen, to a large extent, contradicts most of the popular guidelines set forth by the nutritional and medical communities. The regimen appropriate for acid (and mixed) metabolizers is purine-rich, modest in fat, and seeks to limit carbohydrate intake. As I stated repeatedly in my first book, this regimen can be disastrous for alkaline metabolizers. It is, however, the only nutritional remedy which will ease the distress of acid metabolizers. Gloria's case will provide a powerful example.

Gloria was 49 years old and complained of recurring migraine headaches and chronic anxiety. Unlike many other individuals in industrial societies, Gloria was not overweight but, rather, had problems keeping weight on. Almost 15 pounds underweight, she was unattractively skinny despite the fact that she consumed a great deal of food. She unsuccessfully tried a host of therapies. At the time she discovered BioBalance Therapy she had just gone through menopause and had resigned herself to taking anti-anxiety medication on a regular basis. She had been taking 0.25 milligrams of Xanax, 4 times daily. Xanax is a commonly prescribed anti-anxiety medication that is usually effective in countering panic attacks.

Most notably, prior to initiating her program of BioBalance Therapy, Gloria suffered a particularly nasty reaction to a nutritional regimen recommended by her doctor's nutritionist. Gloria's holistic physician had correctly diagnosed Gloria's condition as hypoglycemia on the basis of the fact that he felt Gloria suffered from "classic hypoglycemic symptoms." (In Chapter 8, you'll see why "classic hypoglycemic symptoms" do not always correctly manifest hypoglycemia, but in this case the doctor got lucky). Unfortunately, Gloria's physician lacked a full understanding of metabolic types and how they react to hypoglycemic conditions. He, therefore, allowed his nutritionist to prescribe a diet, which would exacerbate Gloria's problems rather than solve them.

Specifically, Gloria was told to adhere to a diet consisting primarily of foods rich in complex carbohydrates. She was told that complex carbohydrates (vs. simple carbohydrates) would gradually raise and sustain her blood sugar levels at a normal range. The nutritionist told Gloria that her hypoglycemia put her at high risk for diabetes, and that the prescribed high complex carbohydrate diet would reduce the odds of not becoming diabetic. Chapter Eight explains why this reasoning is incorrect for acid types, and is especially destructive when applied to hypoglycemics like Gloria.

Sure enough, upon follow-up consultation, Gloria reported feeling worse. Her physician then concluded that she was also suffering "classic symptoms" of candidiasis. He subsequently prescribed candicidals (yeast killing medications) in addition to further restricting the diet prescribed by his nutritionist.

When Gloria reported again that she did not respond well to the prescribed candicidals, she was told to be patient because she was suffering a *discharge reaction* (also known as the *Herxheimer reaction*), and that she would feel worse before feeling better. Chapter 8 outlines the need for physicians to institute a careful procedure to avoid making this type of error resulting in misdiagnosis and mistreatment of their patients.

Even though nutritional and medical communities typically view the type of diet prescribed by Gloria's nutritionist as "sensible" and "wholesome," her case illustrates how this type of diet can have disastrous consequences when applied to acid metabolizers. The high complex carbohydrate regimen that Gloria's nutritionist prescribed bears some resemblance to the regimen appropriate for Myra, an alkaline metabolizer, and Gloria's metabolic opposite. Consequently, this diet served to accentuate Gloria's underlying metabolic acid imbalance thereby worsening her condition.

After reading my first book, Gloria realized immediately that she was metabolizing in nonalkaline fashion, and that she was very likely an acid metabolizer. She courageously set one day aside to self-administer the acid-inducing challenge meals. Her November 3rd food-mood diary given below shows the extent of her negative reaction to the food challenge.

Remember my caution that one should never introduce the supplements appropriate for alkaline metabolizers as part of the food challenge meals until after metabolic type has been clearly identified. Given the severity of Gloria's adverse reaction to her acid-inducing challenge meals alone, you can imagine how disastrous her reaction would have been if she had taken the acid-inducing supplements on the day of her challenge test. Let me re-emphasize the fact that BioBalance Therapy when applied correctly or incorrectly is formidably powerful in its capacity to either heal or cause distress.

Gloria's reactions as recorded in her food/mood diary on the day of her challenge meals (appropriate only for alkaline types - no supplements were taken this day) clearly illustrate this.

Food-Mood Diary from Food Challenge Test Day

NAME: *Gloria R.*   DATE: *November 3, 2000*

PHASE OF MENSTRUAL CYCLE:

__ MENSTRUAL   (DAYS 1- 4)

__ PREOVULATORY   (DAYS 5-14)

__ PREMENSTRUAL   (DAYS 15-28)

X   NO CYCLE

Time Upon Arising: *awakened at 4:00 am - nervous - couldn't get back to sleep, finally got out of bed at 5:30 am*

Sleep Description: *4 hours broken sleep, very poor*

Mood Upon Arising: *nervous, apprehensive about trying to stay off medication today so I can see how I respond to challenge foods*

Time of Breakfast: *6:00 am*

Breakfast: *1 cup of regular coffee, 1 glass orange juice, 2 rice cakes*

Mood After Breakfast: *INSTANT PANIC after coffee, I forced the rest of the food down, feel very "choky" - took 0.50 mg Xanax (double my regularly scheduled dose)*

Mood Before Snack: *very edgy, trying not to take any more Xanax*

Midmorning Snack: *none*

Mood After Snack: *still very edgy, almost hyper*

Mood Before Lunch: *hands trembling*

Time of Lunch: 11:30 am

Lunch: Salad with tomatoes, cucumbers, lettuce, Vidalia onions, radishes and sweet peppers + 1 teaspoon extra virgin organic cold pressed olive oil and squeezed lemon, 6 ounces of low fat (1%) yogurt with organic apples, strawberries and blueberries, 1 cup herbal tea

Mood After Lunch: PANIC VERY BAD, took another 0.50 mg Xanax (double dose again); hyperventilating; I feel like I'm going to claw my way out of my skin. Entire upper body trembling before Xanax. Torso buzzing. Head throbbing.

Mood Before Snack: extremely nervous and tense, broke down and cried uncontrollably.

Midafternoon Snack: none

Mood After Snack: same

Mood Before Dinner: buzzing, feeling really hyper, hear a high pitched whining sound in my ears, migraine setting in, extremely tense, cried some more.

Time of Dinner: 5:30 pm

Dinner: fillet of sole, short grain brown rice, baked potato and broccoli, herbal tea with lemon

Mood After Dinner: PANIC AGAIN, took another Xanax (0.50 mgs = double dose)

Mood Before Retiring: awful, very shaky and jumpy, need more Xanax, migraine full blown, can't sleep, hate living this way. Lay in the dark. Saw lights flashing even though my eyes were closed. Almost feel like I'm beginning to hallucinate.

Time of Retiring: 12:30 am

Clearly, Gloria's adverse reactions were the result of her having eaten foods completely inappropriate for her metabolic type. The acid-inducing challenge meals she ate increasingly acidified Gloria's underlying acid imbalance and worsened her symptom severity. Given her adverse reactions, it's my guess that Gloria would very possibly have experienced a full-blown psychotic episode if she had also taken the full course of supplements appropriate for alkaline metabolizers on the day of her food challenge test.

The next set of diaries represents Gloria's progress during her initial recovery through the BioBalance program. The entries for November 4th through the 10th are representative of Gloria's progress during the initial stage of the program prior to taking any supplements. At this point she still did not know whether she was an acid or mixed metabolizer. Gloria ultimately concluded she was probably not metabolically cycling since she was postmenopausal and didn't experience any significant variation in symptom intensity over time. Her levels of distress were about the same, day after day regardless of the time of month or year.

Note from the diaries that Gloria experimented with her regimen to determine whether she was an acid or mixed metabolizer during the November 4th through 10th period. She did this by gauging her reaction to both the regimen appropriate for acid metabolizers and the regimen appropriate for mixed metabolizers. The regimen appropriate for mixed metabolizers is really a combination of the regimen appropriate for acid metabolizers and the regimen appropriate for alkaline metabolizers. It is, however, strongly biased in favor of the regimen appropriate for acid metabolizers. In this regard, mixed metabolizers far more closely resemble acid metabolizers than they do alkaline metabolizers.

Recall that when we reviewed Myra's (alkaline metabolizer) regimen in the last chapter, the key words in describing that regimen were light, purine-poor cuisine. Conversely, and not surprisingly, the key words that I might use in describing the diet appropriate for acid metabolizers are heavy, purine-rich cuisine. You can readily see why this type of nutritional regimen falls into disfavor with our culture, which assumes that the population is metabolically homogenous, and has equated eating "light" to eating right. Once again, while eating light is indeed appropriate for some people—usually alkaline metabolizers—it can be devastating for others. Additionally, I must re-emphasize that proteins alone are insufficient in correcting Gloria's underlying acid imbalance, if those proteins are not purines or nucleoproteins.

Gloria's Food/Mood Diaries — Day 1

NAME: *Gloria R.*   DATE: *November 4, 2000*
PHASE OF MENSTRUAL CYCLE:
___ MENSTRUAL   (DAYS 1- 4)
___ PREOVULATORY   (DAYS 5-14)
___ PREMENSTRUAL   (DAYS 15-28)
X NO CYCLE

Time at Arising: *3:45 am couldn't get back to sleep, finally got up at 5:00 am*
Sleep Description: *very poor*
Mood Upon Arising: *nervous, took 1 Xanax (0.25 mgs), hopeful that the diet that's right for acid types which I'll try today will help*

Time of Breakfast: *5:30 am*
Breakfast: *2 ounces of hamburger, 2 strips of bacon, buttered bread, weak tea with half and half*
Mood After Breakfast: *less nervous, but still not too good*

Mood Before Snack: *increasing nervousness, trying to resist taking a Xanax*
Midmorning Snack: *diet thin bread with generous amount of peanut butter, cup of homemade beef broth incompletely skimmed (some fat on surface)*
Mood After Snack: *better, but not good*

Mood Before Lunch: *hungry, feel like migraine is coming on*
Time of Lunch: *11:30 am*

Lunch: sardines in olive oil, creamy new England clam chowder soup with lots of clams
Mood After Lunch: migraine going away, hunger satisfied, less nervous but not good

---

Mood Before Snack: hungry again, getting very nervous, took 1 Xanax
Midafternoon Snack: cup of bean with bacon soup with lots of bacon
Mood After Snack: a little better

Mood Before Dinner: hungry, tired and a little nervous
Time of Dinner: 5:30 pm
Dinner: chicken liver sautéed in butter, fried cauliflower, steamed carrots in butter, herbal tea with half and half
Mood After Dinner: not great but better than I've felt all day

---

Mood Before Retiring: a little hopeful, only took two Xanax today, usually take 4
Time of Retiring: 12:30 am

Gloria's Food/Mood Diaries — Day 2

NAME: Gloria R.   DATE: November 5, 2000
PHASE OF MENSTRUAL CYCLE:
__ MENSTRUAL   (DAYS 1- 4)
__ PREOVULATORY   (DAYS 5-14)
__ PREMENSTRUAL   (DAYS 15-28)
X NO CYCLE

Time at Arising: 5:00 am
Sleep Description: 4 1/2 hour, poor but not as broken as usual

Mood Upon Arising: *nervous, hungry and cold, took a Xanax (will continue with diet that's right for acid types today)*

Time of Breakfast: *6:00 am*
Breakfast: *pork sausage, hash browns cooked in butter, fried egg*
Mood After Breakfast: *hunger gone, feel warmer, less nervous*

Mood Before Snack: *hungry and more nervous*
Midmorning Snack: *leftover pork sausage and hash browns*
Mood After Snack: *better*

Mood Before Lunch: *hungry, tired and a little nervous*
Time of Lunch: *11:30 am*
Lunch: *canned salmon, artichoke hearts and mushroom caps in olive oil, 1 slice diet bread*
Mood After Lunch: *better, seemed to calm down a bit (maybe my imagination)*

Mood Before Snack: *getting nervous again*
Midafternoon Snack: *nothing available (out shopping)*
Mood After Snack: *extremely nervous took Xanax - don't go without snacks any more!*

Mood Before Dinner: *exhausted*
Time of Dinner: *5:30 pm*
Dinner: *rib steak, corn on the cob with butter, cream of spinach soup, herbal tea with half and half*

Mood After Dinner: *better than I've felt all day but not great*

Mood Before Retiring: *tired, snacked on cashew butter on rice cake*

Time of Retiring: *12:00 am*

Gloria's Food/Mood Diaries — Day 3

NAME: *Gloria R.*   DATE: *November 6, 2000*

PHASE OF MENSTRUAL CYCLE:

__ MENSTRUAL   (DAYS 1- 4)

__ PREOVULATORY   (DAYS 5-14)

__ PREMENSTRUAL   (DAYS 15-28)

X NO CYCLE

Time at Arising: *5:30 pm*

Sleep Description: *5 1/2 hours not good but not as broken as usual*

Mood Upon Arising: *somewhat nervous, first time in a long time I feel like I can go without my "wake up Xanax"*

Time of Breakfast: *6:00 am*

Breakfast: *fried pork chop, fried egg in butter, weak herbal tea with half and half*

Mood After Breakfast: *steady mood, slight headache*

Mood Before Snack: *hungry, headache gone*

Midmorning Snack: *rice cake with thick slab of almond butter, weak herbal tea*

Mood After Snack: *ok . . . but just barely ok*

Mood Before Lunch: *same*

Time of Lunch: *11:30 am*

Lunch: *chicken thigh and drumstick with creamed corn and butter*

Mood After Lunch: *a little better*

Mood Before Snack: getting jittery and jumpy again, took a Xanax
Midafternoon Snack: leftover pork chop from breakfast
Mood After Snack: calmer

Mood Before Dinner: getting nervous
Time of Dinner: 5:30 pm
Dinner: roast beef, roast potatoes with gravy from roast beef, asparagus with butter
Mood After Dinner: calmer

Mood Before Retiring: hopeful and tired, unusual for me in that I'm always too wound up to be tired
Time of Retiring: 11:00 pm

Gloria's Food/Mood Diaries — Day 4

NAME: Gloria R.   DATE: November 7, 2000
PHASE OF MENSTRUAL CYCLE:
__ MENSTRUAL   (DAYS 1- 4)
__ PREOVULATORY   (DAYS 5-14)
__ PREMENSTRUAL   (DAYS 15-28)
X NO CYCLE

Time at Arising: 5:00 am
Sleep Description: better than usual, only got up twice to urinate
Mood Upon Arising: still hopeful (will stay on diet right for acid types), no need for "wake up Xanax"

Time of Breakfast: 5:30 am
Breakfast: corned beef hash with egg, 1 slice of diet thin toast with butter

Mood After Breakfast: ok, somewhat steadier than usual

Mood Before Snack: getting a bit antsy
Midmorning Snack: rich partially de-fatted chicken soup with chunks of dark meat chicken
Mood After Snack: less antsy

Mood Before Lunch: getting hungry again
Time of Lunch: 11:30 am
Lunch: red sock-eye salmon with small amount of whole mayonnaise and chopped celery, spinach salad with kidney beans and string beans in olive oil dressing
Mood After Lunch: better, seem to feel a little calmer

Mood Before Snack: getting nervous again, feel like I could use a xanax, trying to resist
Midafternoon Snack: leftover salmon salad, rice cake with butter
Mood After Snack: better

Mood Before Dinner: same
Time of Dinner: 6:00 pm
Dinner: 6 large scallops sauteed in butter, buttered lima beans, creamed corn niblets, weak tea
Mood After Dinner: better than I've felt all day. For the first time in almost 9 months I haven't taken a Xanax - HURRAY!

Mood Before Retiring: very hopeful and sleepy
Time of Retiring: 11:00 pm

Gloria's Food/Mood Diaries — Day 5

NAME: Gloria R.   DATE: November 8, 2000
PHASE OF MENSTRUAL CYCLE:
__ MENSTRUAL   (DAYS 1- 4)
__ PREOVULATORY   (DAYS 5-14)
__ PREMENSTRUAL   (DAYS 15-28)
X NO CYCLE

Time at Arising: 6:30 am
Sleep Description: 7 1/2 hours, awakened only once at
   2:30. Was a little nervous but ws able to get
   back to sleep, otherwise pretty good for me
Mood Upon Arising: reasonably calm (will stick with
   diet right for acid types today)

Time of Breakfast: 7:00 am
Breakfast: lamb patty, whole oats with heavy cream
Mood After Breakfast: steady

Mood Before Snack: getting nervous
Midmorning Snack: thick slab of almond butter
   on rice cake
Mood After Snack: better

Mood Before Lunch: ok but hungry
Time of Lunch: 11:30 am
Lunch: bacon cheeseburger (no dressing), french
   fries (out shopping)
Mood After Lunch: ok

Mood Before Snack: getting nervous, resisting taking a
   Xanax
Midafternoon Snack: 1/2 an apple with thick slab of
   cashew butter, weak herbal tea

Mood After Snack: *better*

Mood Before Dinner: getting hungry and nervous
Time of Dinner: 5:30 pm
Dinner: home made beef stroganoff (big chunks of
   beef, and easy on the noodles), bean with bacon
   soup, mashed potatoes with butter and beef
   gravy, small taste of ice cream for dessert
Mood After Dinner: pretty good

Mood Before Retiring: sleepy but jubilant, second day
   and no Xanax, not easy but I'm doing it! Also,
   no migraines for almost 3 days!
Time of Retiring: 11:00 pm

Gloria's Food/Mood Diaries — Day 6

NAME: Gloria R.   DATE: November 9, 2000
PHASE OF MENSTRUAL CYCLE:
__ MENSTRUAL   (DAYS 1- 4)
__ PREOVULATORY   (DAYS 5-14)
__ PREMENSTRUAL   (DAYS 15-28)
X NO CYCLE

Time at Arising: 6:30 am
Sleep Description: 7 1/2 hours, slept almost all night
Mood Upon Arising: not bad, no need for "wake up xanax"
   (will experiment with diet that's right for mixed
   types today)

Time of Breakfast: 7:00 am
Breakfast: bacon and eggs, weak
   coffee with 1% milk
Mood After Breakfast: pretty good

Mood Before Snack: *getting nervous*
Midmorning Snack: *1 organic apple*
Mood After Snack: *not too good*

Mood Before Lunch: *uneasy*
Time of Lunch: *11:30 am*
Lunch: *dark and light meat chicken salad with diced onions and peppers with mixture low fat yogurt and low fat mayonnaise, rye bread and tea with lemon*
Mood After Lunch: *PANIC! Took a Xanax*

Mood Before Snack: *worst than I've felt in days*
Midafternoon Snack: *sardines in olive oil with a little squeezed lemon*
Mood After Snack: *better*

Mood Before Dinner: *so-so*
Time of Dinner: *6:00 pm*
Dinner: *Pork loin with string beans, mashed potatoes and gravy*
Mood After Dinner: *better*

Mood Before Retiring: *a little nervous, resisting taking a Xanax, I don't think I'm mixed, I must be acid.*
Time of Retiring: *11:30 pm*

Gloria's Food/Mood Diaries — Day 7

NAME: *Gloria R.*   DATE: *November 10, 2000*
PHASE OF MENSTRUAL CYCLE:
__ MENSTRUAL   (DAYS 1- 4)
__ PREOVULATORY   (DAYS 5-14)
__ PREMENSTRUAL   (DAYS 15-28)
X NO CYCLE

Time at Arising: *5:30 am*
Sleep Description: *6 hours, not too bad*
Mood Upon Arising: *ok (will go back to regimen for acid types)*

Time of Breakfast: *6:00 am*
Breakfast: *hamburger and fried egg, weak herbal tea with half and half*
Mood After Breakfast: *ok*

Mood Before Snack: *getting a little nervous*
Midmorning Snack: *banana with thick slab of almond butter*
Mood After Snack: *a little better*

Mood Before Lunch: *ok*
Time of Lunch: *11:30 am*
Lunch: pot roast, *buttered peas and carrots*
Mood After Lunch: *better*

Mood Before Snack: *getting hungry*
Midafternoon Snack: *cup of rich home made chicken soup (not completely de-fatted), rice cake*
Mood After Snack: *pretty good*

Mood Before Dinner: *a little wound up*
Time of Dinner: *6:00 pm*
Dinner: *calf liver sautéed in butter with sautéed mushrooms caps, fried cauliflower and carrots, weak herbal tea*
Mood After Dinner: *much better*

Mood Before Retiring: *calmer, feeling like I'm gaining lost ground, and I've also gained almost 7 pounds!*
Time of Retiring: *11:00 pm*

You can see how the alterations in Gloria's diet changed her levels of anxiety. The heavy nutritional regimen (again, the diametric opposite of Myra's regimen in the previous chapter) seemed to agree with Gloria. Making this heavy regimen a bit lighter by introducing some foods appropriate only for alkaline metabolizers such as coffee, low fat milk, low fat yogurt, chicken breast, etc., makes the resultant combination appropriate for mixed metabolizers. Gloria clearly had an adverse reaction to the light/heavy mixed combination, again proving her to be an acid metabolizer.

The next set of diaries dated December 19th through December 23rd lets you track Gloria through the final phase of BioBalance Therapy where she introduced vitamin/mineral supplements. Once again, I would urge you to refer to the appendix for details. Gloria experimented for a second time with the possibility that her well-being might in fact be optimized if she ate the heavy regimen appropriate for acid metabolizers in combination with the companion set of vitamins and minerals appropriate for mixed metabolizers. She discovered that she reacted adversely to this combination, and discovered as well that she could remain relatively symptom-free by eating foods appropriate *only* for acid metabolizers, and by taking *only* the supplements appropriate for acid metabolizers. In fact, she found that her supplements helped sustain her throughout the day to the point where she no longer needed to eat between meal snacks as frequently as she had previously. Recall that in the previous chapter, Myra also found that she had to alter her diet to compensate for her supplements. In Myra's case she found that she could no longer drink coffee with impunity after she started taking her supplements. Gloria discovered that she metabolized foods in an extremely acid mode, and that she could tolerate three full doses of supplements appropriate for acid metabolizers daily, one dose after each meal. It turned out that Gloria's after-dinner dose of supplements helped her sleep through the night without interruption.

Gloria's Food/Mood Diaries With Supplements

Note: Gloria tested her nutritional regimen for approximately one month without supplements before introducing the supplemental vitamins and minerals appropriate for her metabolic type.

Gloria's Food/Mood Diaries — Day 1

NAME: *Gloria R.*   DATE: *December 19, 2000*
PHASE OF MENSTRUAL CYCLE:
__ MENSTRUAL   (DAYS 1- 4)
__ PREOVULATORY   (DAYS 5-14)
__ PREMENSTRUAL   (DAYS 15-28)
X   NO CYCLE

Time at Arising: *7:00 am*
Sleep Description: *6 hours, not bad, awakened only twice*
Mood Upon Arising: *ok, a little nervous, but still*
    hopeful, have taken only 12 Xanax over the
    past month when I would normally take more
    than 120 (4 a day) - I'm going to start
    taking the supplements appropriate for acid
    types today, a full dose after each meal.

Time of Breakfast: *7:30 am*
Breakfast: *sausage and fried egg, weak tea*
Mood After Breakfast: *pretty good*

Mood Before Snack: *still steady*
Midmorning Snack: *rice cake and peanut butter*
Mood After Snack: *still good*

Mood Before Lunch: *same*
Time of Lunch: *12:00 pm*

Lunch: *tuna noodle casserole with dark meat tuna in oil (i.e., "chunk light" not "fancy white albacore"), easy on the noodles with buttered peas and heavy cream sauce, cup of New England clam chowder*
Mood After Lunch: *centered*

Mood Before Snack: *still good*
Midafternoon Snack: *not hungry, I'll try skipping it*
Mood After Snack: *same*

Mood Before Dinner: *a bit hungry but not too bad*
Time of Dinner: *6:30 pm*
Dinner: *fried chicken thigh and drumstick, buttered peas and carrots*
Mood After Dinner: *calm*

Mood Before Retiring: *calm and sleepy*
Time of Retiring: *10:30 pm*

Gloria's Food/Mood Diaries — Day 2

NAME: *Gloria R.*   DATE: *December 20, 2000*
PHASE OF MENSTRUAL CYCLE:
__ MENSTRUAL   (DAYS 1- 4)
__ PREOVULATORY   (DAYS 5-14)
__ PREMENSTRUAL   (DAYS 15-28)
X   NO CYCLE

Time at Arising: *7:00 am*
Sleep Description: *better than I can recall in a long time*
Mood Upon Arising: *calm and a bit hungry*

Time of Breakfast: 8:00 am
Breakfast: corned beef hash and egg fried in
 butter, a little egg nog
Mood After Breakfast: pretty good

Mood Before Snack: fine, not too hungry
Midmorning Snack: none
Mood After Snack: same

Mood Before Lunch: a little hungry
Time of Lunch: 1:00 pm
Lunch: salmon and anchovy salad consisting of
 salmon, artichoke hearts, boiled potatoes (easy
 on the potatoes), kidney beans, anchovies and
 olive oil, weak herbal tea
Mood After Lunch: centered

Mood Before Snack: same
Midafternoon Snack: rice cake and thick slab of cashew
 butter
Mood After Snack: cheerful and energetic

Mood Before Dinner: same
Time of Dinner: 7:00 pm
Dinner: steamed clams with butter, sautéed
 scallops, buttered corn and string beans, taste
 of chocolate ice cream, weak herbal tea
Mood After Dinner: calm

Mood Before Retiring: calm and sleepy
Time of Retiring: 10:30 pm

Gloria's Food/Mood Diaries — Day 3

NAME: Gloria R.   DATE: December 21, 2000
PHASE OF MENSTRUAL CYCLE:
__ MENSTRUAL   (DAYS 1- 4)
__ PREOVULATORY   (DAYS 5-14)
__ PREMENSTRUAL   (DAYS 15-28)
X NO CYCLE

Time at Arising: 6:30 am
Sleep Description: 8 hours, deep sleep
Mood Upon Arising: calm, centered

Time of Breakfast: 7:30 am
Breakfast: bacon and refried beans, 1 slice diet thin
    bread and weak tea
Mood After Breakfast: good, relaxed

Mood Before Snack: same
Midmorning Snack: leftover bacon from
    breakfast on pita bread
Mood After Snack: good

Mood Before Lunch: same
Time of Lunch: 1:00 pm
Lunch: hamburger and french fries (out shopping)
Mood After Lunch: good, calm

Mood Before Snack: same
Midafternoon Snack: none
Mood After Snack: same

Mood Before Dinner: somewhat hungry but not too bad
Time of Dinner: 6:30 pm
Dinner: lamb chops, mashed cauliflower with butter
    and grated cheese, lima beans, weak tea

Mood After Dinner: relaxed

Mood Before Retiring: relaxed and sleepy
Time of Retiring: 10:00 pm

Gloria's Food/Mood Diaries — Day 4

NAME: Gloria R.   DATE: December 22 2000
PHASE OF MENSTRUAL CYCLE:
__ MENSTRUAL   (DAYS 1- 4)
__ PREOVULATORY   (DAYS 5-14)
__ PREMENSTRUAL   (DAYS 15-28)
X NO CYCLE

Time at Arising: 7:00 am
Sleep Description: 9 hours deep sleep, awakened once
    to go to bathroom
Mood Upon Arising: calm, relaxed. Will try eating
    foods right for acid types but will take
    vitamin/mineral supplements appropriate for
    mixed types today instead of supplements for
    acid types to see if I can do better still

Time of Breakfast: 7:30 am
Breakfast: ham and scrambled eggs with Swiss
    cheese weak tea
Mood After Breakfast: still good

Mood Before Snack: somewhat hungry
Midmorning Snack: 1/2 apple with almond butter
Mood After Snack: hungrier and a little nauseous

Mood Before Lunch: very hungry and a little shaky,
    feel like panic attack may be coming on.
Time of Lunch: 11:30 am

Lunch: dark turkey meat on buttered rye, cream of spinach soup, herbal tea
Mood After Lunch: getting wound up again, RESUME SUPPLEMENTS APPROPRIATE FOR ACID TYPES

Mood Before Snack: feeling like I could use a Xanax again, I really don't like this
Midafternoon Snack: cup of home made turkey broth with rich stock and some dark meat turkey
Mood After Snack: a little better

Mood Before Dinner: somewhat tired
Time of Dinner: 6:00 pm
Dinner: turkey thigh and drumstick with gravy, succotash (buttered corn and lima beans), weak herbal tea
Mood After Dinner: calm but exhausted, feel like crying

Mood Before Retiring: very tired
Time of Retiring: 9:30 pm

Gloria's Food/Mood Diaries — Day 5

NAME: Gloria R.   DATE: December 23, 2000
PHASE OF MENSTRUAL CYCLE:
__ MENSTRUAL   (DAYS 1- 4)
__ PREOVULATORY   (DAYS 5-14)
__ PREMENSTRUAL   (DAYS 15-28)
X   NO CYCLE

Time at Arising: 5:30 am
Sleep Description: ok
Mood Upon Arising: a bit weary. Will stick to 3 full doses of supplements appropriate only for acid types from here on.

112

Time of Breakfast: 6:30 am
Breakfast: hamburger and mushrooms fried in butter
    with rice cake
Mood After Breakfast: much improved

Mood Before Snack: centered
Midmorning Snack: none
Mood After Snack: same

Mood Before Lunch: same
Time of Lunch: 12:30 pm
Lunch: shrimp salad with mayonnaise and chopped
    celery in avocado, three bean salad with olive oil
Mood After Lunch: cheerful and relaxed

Mood Before Snack: good
Midafternoon Snack: none
Mood After Snack: good

Mood Before Dinner: getting a bit hungry
Time of Dinner: 6:30 pm
Dinner: liver pate (home made), baked potato with
    butter and sour cream
Mood After Dinner: tranquil

Mood Before Retiring: sleepy but good
Time of Retiring: 10:30 pm

Before ending this chapter, I'd like to give you a sample week-long
menu of foods appropriate for acid metabolizers. The seven-day menu
listed below should give you a specific idea as to how an acid metabolizer
must eat in order to achieve and maintain a state of BioBalance. Once
again, you may create your own menu provided you do so within the
nutritional guidelines provided in the appendix.

As stated in my first book, acid metabolizers must eat meat, fish and poultry of the "allowed" varieties at every meal (see the appendix). *Insofar as acid metabolizers are concerned, any meal without allowed meat, fish and poultry is simply not a meal.* Let me once again comment on the modern day taboo against eating excessive animal foods and fats. The simple fact of the matter is that acid metabolizers are oxidizing (burning up) glucose (blood sugar) at such a prodigious rate that they need the type of regimen recommended in this book if they are to buffer their biochemistry against repeated acid shock which is the primary cause of their distress.

Incidentally, don't make the error of thinking that an individual who burns up blood sugar rapidly needs extra sugar or even complex carbohydrates to offset this defect. Recently, the medical community has irresponsibly been telling people who burn up blood sugar too rapidly and therefore suffer from chronic low blood sugar (known as "hypoglycemia"), to rely upon complex carbohydrates. Physicians who prescribe nutritional therapy in so irresponsible a fashion are unwittingly sentencing their acid patients to ever-deepening suffering and despair, because increased consumption of carbohydrates (simple or complex) will increase the rate at which blood sugar is burned up. Unfortunately, many individuals classified as "hypoglycemic" by well-meaning physicians are not hypoglycemic at all because the medically accepted test for hypoglycemia (the glucose tolerance test) is unreliable. If you want to know more about blood sugar related problems, namely hypoglycemia and diabetes, you will find additional information in Chapter 8.

While I don't list snacks below, snacks are important for acid metabolizers. Appropriate snacks consist of nut butters (especially peanut butter), nuts and seeds, and rich homemade beef, chicken or turkey stock. A piece of fruit as a snack by itself is completely inappropriate for acid metabolizers and will intensify symptom severity.

Sample One Week Menu Appropriate for Acid Types

Here's a sample of how an acid metabolizer might eat during a seven-day period.

Day 1

Breakfast: Bacon and egg(s) (eggs optional), thin sliced toast with butter, decaffeinated coffee with half and half.

Lunch: New England clam chowder; dark meat tuna packed in oil ("chunk light" tuna - not "solid white fancy albacore" tuna) with mayonnaise and chopped celery on diet thin bread, weak herbal tea (any decaffeinated variety).

Dinner: Rib steak, buttered corn, peas and carrots, weak herbal tea (any variety).

Day 2

Breakfast: Hamburger patty and egg(s) (eggs optional), home fried potatoes, decaffeinated tea.

Lunch: Split pea soup with ham, mild chili with beef, weak herbal tea (any variety).

Dinner: Chicken thigh and/or drumstick, asparagus tips, fried brown rice, weak herbal tea (any variety).

Day 3

Breakfast: Sausage and egg(s) (eggs optional), thin toast, decaffeinated tea

Lunch: Sardine sandwich (preferably sardines packed in oil) on thin sliced bread, weak herbal tea (any variety).

Dinner: Broiled salmon with drawn butter, creamed corn, carrots, weak herbal tea (any variety), weak herbal tea (any variety).

Day 4

Breakfast: Kippers (smoked herring) and egg(s) (eggs optional), weak herbal tea (any variety).

Lunch: Bean with bacon soup, roast beef sandwich (no dressing), weak herbal tea (any variety).

Dinner: Liver paté, spinach salad with artichoke hearts, beans (any variety) and asparagus tips, olive oil dressing, weak herbal tea (any variety).

Day 5

Breakfast: Corned beef hash and egg(s) (eggs optional), thin toast with butter, decaffeinated coffee with half and half.

Lunch: Chicken salad sandwich with dark meat chicken only (thigh or drumstick), dressing to consist of mayonnaise and chopped celery, weak herbal tea (any variety).

Dinner: Pan fried liver (any variety), sautéed mushrooms and fried rice, fried cauliflower, weak herbal tea (any variety).

Day 6

Breakfast: Lamb patty and egg(s) (eggs optional), weak herbal tea (any variety).

Lunch: Tuna salad with: chunk light tuna packed in oil (not white tuna), on leaf spinach, artichoke hearts, assorted beans (waxed, lima beans, string beans, etc.); dressing to consist of olive oil and small amount of fresh squeezed lemon (for flavor if desired), weak herbal tea (any variety).

Dinner: Pot roast, buttered corn on the cob, peas and carrots, weak herbal tea (any variety).

Day 7

Breakfast: Smoked salmon and eggs, weak herbal tea (any variety).

Lunch: Bacon cheeseburger, french fries, weak herbal tea (any variety).

Dinner: Leg of lamb, mashed potatoes with gravy, creamed spinach, weak herbal tea (any variety).

Chapter Two provides you with additional information on important variations of the regimen appropriate for acid metabolizers. Gloria did ultimately use these variations for a period of the time. She found that supplementing her meals with whole grains such as brown rice, barley and millet helped ease some mild and occasional bouts of constipation. She did not adhere to this premier variation steadfastly, however, but did eat dark meat and organ meat derived from free ranging, organically fed poultry on those occasions when she chose not to eat seafood. On relatively infrequent occasions when she ate out, she either ate allowed seafood or whatever allowed meats were available.

6

Paul H. — A Mixed Mode Metabolizer:

This chapter introduces you to Paul H., a mixed mode metabolizer. Mixed mode metabolizers are a combination of acid and alkaline metabolizers, biased substantially in favor of their acid counterparts. So if a mixed metabolizer errs in formulating her/his nutritional regimen, that error should favor the selection of foods appropriate for acid metabolizers. As a general rule of thumb, the ideal acid to alkaline ratio for foods will range from 2:1 to 4:1, depending on the individual. Roughly speaking, mixed types should select about 2/3rds of their food items from the categories listed as recommended for acid metabolizers.

This mixture may at first glance seem more difficult to achieve than it actually is. Virtually every mixed metabolizer I've dealt with has had a reasonably good sense of where to draw the line. Let me provide you with an analogy that will give you some peace of mind if you are a mixed metabolizer and are fearful of making an inappropriate selection. The nutritional path you must take as a mixed metabolizer resembles that of a multi-lane super highway far more so than a tightrope. If you steer clear of the center median and the shoulder of the road, you will be in reasonably good shape. BioBalance is just as the name says, a process of building balance. You need not fear that small, experimental or adjusting deviations in your mix will result in catastrophic reactions. The examples provided in this chapter give a clearer idea of what I'm talking about.

Although a mixed metabolizer is better off erring in favor of the regimen appropriate for acid metabolizers, this advice should not be taken to extreme. It would be wrong to think that if a 4:1 mix is acceptable, then a 10:1 mix must be even better. I've seen cases where mixed metabolizers reason as follows: "the vitamin/mineral supplements appropriate for mixed metabolizers are different than the supplements appropriate for acid metabolizers, so if I eat only the foods appropriate for acid metabolizers and take the supplements that are right for mixed metabolizers, I should do okay in the long run." This type of reasoning is incorrect, as you will see from Paul's diaries below. The regimen appropriate for acid metabolizers serves to correct severe acid metabolic imbalances. That regimen is therefore highly alkaline-inducing. While mixed metabolizers tend to be somewhat acidic, they are not acidic to the extent that they can comfortably eat only those foods appropriate for acid metabolizers. They must mix both regimens in the manner described here.

I have also observed that mixed metabolizers generally fall into the following two categories:

- Individuals who may eat a relatively light breakfast (free of purine-rich meats, fish and/or poultry), but who must nevertheless eat purine-rich meats, fish or poultry for both lunch and dinner.
- Individuals who must eat purine-rich meats, fish and/or poultry for breakfast, lunch and dinner.

Straightforward trial-and-error is the only way to make this determination on an individual-specific basis. I'll provide sample menus at the end of this chapter showing you how each subclass might eat.

Paul H. is 58 years old. His list of symptoms included chronic and worsening irascibility, an all around "lousy personality" (as his wife, Fran described him), and a skin rash which had repeatedly been diagnosed as "stress related." His wife also described Paul as "extremely childish," "dependent," "petulant," at times "downright mean," and claimed that he would "blow up" at her for no apparent reason. During more lucid moments Paul himself had come to conclude that his wife typically had little if anything to do with his episodes of hostility. He stated, "I just can't help myself about my anger. It's sort of like an itch. When it itches - I gotta scratch."

Fran was the key factor in getting her husband Paul into BioBalance Therapy. She had read my first book, deciphered her own BioProfile, benefited by eating accordingly, and felt that Paul could benefit as well. More importantly, she feared that Paul might resort to physical abuse if his condition remained unchecked. Paul's physician had suggested that he seek out the assistance of a psychotherapist. Paul decided to get involved in BioBalance Therapy as an alternative to psychotherapy, which he distrusted. His wife also gave him impetus to seek assistance by giving him an ultimatum, "Get help or get a divorce!"

The diary listed below dated March 4th shows Paul's reactions to his acid-inducing challenge meals. You will note that while Paul's reactions were unfavorable, the magnitude of his symptoms was not nearly as great as the magnitude of Gloria's in the preceding chapter. This is to be expected since as a mixed metabolizer, Paul's tendency to deviate toward the acid end of the spectrum is not as great as that of an acid metabolizer such as Gloria. You will also note that despite his adverse reactions throughout the day, Paul did seem to pick up a bit in the evening. This does not imply that Paul is cycling diurnally (throughout the course of the day). Diurnal cycling is actually very rare. Despite eating foods that were inappropriate for his metabolic type on his food challenge day, symptom relief in the early evening in Paul's case is characteristic of a *rebound reaction*, fairly common among mixed metabolizers. This rebound reaction is the result of an *autocompensatory response* among mixed metabolizers which prevents them from straying too far in the acid direction even if they are consuming acid inducing foods. It is not necessary to understand the biochemical basis of this reaction to understand Paul's progress in BioBalance Therapy.

Paul H's Food/Mood Diary on the day of his challenge meals (Without Supplements)

NAME: Paul H..   DATE: March 4, 2001
PHASE OF MENSTRUAL CYCLE:
__ MENSTRUAL   (DAYS 1- 4)
__ PREOVULATORY   (DAYS 5-14)
__ PREMENSTRUAL   (DAYS 15-28)
X   NO CYCLE

Time at Arising: 7:30 am
Sleep Description: ok
Mood Upon Arising: ok

Time of Breakfast: 7:45 am
Breakfast: 1 glass orange juice, 1 cup of coffee,
   1 rice cake
Mood After Breakfast: ok, hate rice cakes, if I gotta
   eat this way to feel good - forget it!

Mood Before Snack: ticked off at Fran for "hiding"
   my golf clubs, skin feels real itchy
Midmorning Snack: none
Mood After Snack: hungry, this diet stinks

Mood Before Lunch: skin still feels itchy even after I
   used the doc's cream, still hungry
Time of Lunch: 12:00 pm
Lunch: salad with cucumbers, onions, radishes,
   lettuce, shredded cabbage and sweet peppers
   low fat yogurt dressing, tea with lemon
Mood After Lunch: ticked off at Fran's relatives,
   they're real morons, this diet stinks, skin feels
   awful, where the hell's my golf clubs?!

Mood Before Snack: no change
Midafternoon Snack: none
Mood After Snack: diets are for women, fat people,
   hypochondriacs, and crazy people. this
   biobalance stuff is just plain stupid!

Mood Before Dinner: if Fran doesn't have my dinner on
   time I think I'm gonna belt her one, where the
   hell's the TV remote control? - I wanna see
   the damn fights tonite
Time of Dinner: 6:30 pm
Dinner: chicken breast, rice, broccoli, stewed
   tomatoes, coffee (decaf)

Mood After Dinner: *ok, a little better, can't believe that I misplaced my golf clubs, sorry to see Fran crying, sometimes I feel like a jerk*

Mood Before Retiring: *ok*

Time of Retiring: *12:00 am*

Of the three possible options for Paul (alkaline, acid or mixed), it's easy to eliminate the alkaline option. As in Gloria's case, it remained for Paul to determine whether he was an acid or mixed metabolizer. Note that he started the next phase of BioBalance Therapy by self-administering the nutritional regimen appropriate for acid metabolizers. Within the first two days, adverse reactions strongly suggested he was not an acid metabolizer. The regimen was making Paul too alkaline (remember, the diet that's right for acid metabolizers is by definition highly alkaline-inducing). Paul's psychological reaction was initially favorable, but short-lived. Paul rapidly shot past a state of BioBalance into the alkaline portion of the acid/alkaline spectrum, and became excessively tired, loggy and fatigued. When he subsequently introduced some acid-inducing foods to more fully conform to his mixed demands his stupor ended and he felt 'back on track.'

On March 7th, Paul's breakfast included some foods appropriate for alkaline metabolizers such as orange juice and coffee. His midmorning snack on that day was therapeutically tilted in the acid-inducing direction to help eliminate a severe fatigue resulting from the alkaline-inducing foods he had for breakfast. You'll also note that while orange juice had therapeutic value in terminating Paul's alkaline-induced state of fatigue, as a mixed metabolizer Paul did not routinely drink orange juice between meals after that. While mixed metabolizers such as Paul may drink orange juice, he learned to do so with other foods, which are alkaline inducing. His breakfast on March 6th and his breakfasts thereafter provide good examples of the appropriate nutritional context within which this food should be consumed by mixed metabolizers.

Paul H's Food/Mood Diary - Day 1

NAME: Paul H..   DATE: March 5, 2001
PHASE OF MENSTRUAL CYCLE:
__ MENSTRUAL   (DAYS 1- 4)
__ PREOVULATORY   (DAYS 5-14)
__ PREMENSTRUAL   (DAYS 15-28)
X NO CYCLE

Time at Arising: 7:30 am
Sleep Description: ok
Mood Upon Arising: ok, skin feels real bad, my doctor's
    an idiot, gotta get another one, where the
    hell's the TV guide - I wonder who the hell
    took it this time!?

Time of Breakfast: 8:00 am
Breakfast: corned beef hash and eggs, toast with
    butter, decaf coffee with half andhalf
Mood After Breakfast: that's what I call great eating!
    Skin's the same

Mood Before Snack: ok, can't believe I left the TV guide in the
    garage
Midmorning Snack: none
Mood After Snack: ok

Mood Before Lunch: a little hungry
Time of Lunch: 12:00 pm
Lunch: bacon cheeseburger, french fries and
    decaf coffee
Mood After Lunch: pretty good, kidding around with Fran

Mood Before Snack: same
Midafternoon Snack: apple with peanut butter
Mood After Snack: tasted ok, feel ok, went for walk

Mood Before Dinner: *not bad*
Time of Dinner: *7:00 pm*
Dinner: *prime rib, buttered corn on the cob, mashed potatoes and gravy*
Mood After Dinner: *great food, feel ok*

Mood Before Retiring: *all right*
Time of Retiring: *11:30 pm*

Paul H's Food/Mood Diary - Day 2

NAME: *Paul H..*   DATE: *March 6, 2001*
PHASE OF MENSTRUAL CYCLE:
__ MENSTRUAL   (DAYS 1- 4)
__ PREOVULATORY   (DAYS 5-14)
__ PREMENSTRUAL   (DAYS 15-28)
X   NO CYCLE

Time at Arising: *10:00 am*
Sleep Description: *9 1/2 hours, feel like I'm drugged, what the hell is this?*
Mood Upon Arising: *tired*

Time of Breakfast: *10:30 am*
Breakfast: *pork sausage and egg, roll with butter, decaf coffee*
Mood After Breakfast: *ok, still tired*

Mood Before Snack: *gotta take a nap (11:45 am)*
Midmorning Snack: *none*
Mood After Snack: *woke up at 12:30 pm*

Mood Before Lunch: *beat, loggy*
Time of Lunch: *1:00 pm*

Lunch: *hot tuna melt (dark meat tuna fish sandwich with melted cheese), celery and carrot sticks*

Mood After Lunch: *ok*

Mood Before Snack: *still beat, what the hell is this*

Midafternoon Snack: *none*

Mood After Snack: *tried playin' golf - game's all off, quit after 5 holes, tired*

Mood Before Dinner: *tired*

Time of Dinner: *7:00 pm*

Dinner: *fried liver with bacon and mushrooms, creamed spinach, tea*

Mood After Dinner: *real tired*

Mood Before Retiring: *exhausted*

Time of Retiring: *9:00 pm*

Paul H's Food/Mood Diary - Day 3

NAME: *Paul H..*   DATE: *March 7, 2001*

PHASE OF MENSTRUAL CYCLE:

__ MENSTRUAL   (DAYS 1- 4)

__ PREOVULATORY   (DAYS 5-14)

__ PREMENSTRUAL   (DAYS 15-28)

X   NO CYCLE

Time at Arising: *7:30 am*

Sleep Description: *10 1/2 hours, drugged sleep*

Mood Upon Arising: *sleepy but a little better after taking a shower*

Time of Breakfast
Breakfast: 1 glass orange juice, 1 sausage link with home fries, 1 cup weak coffee (not decaf), lots of water
Mood After Breakfast: tired but seem to be picking up a little

Mood Before Snack: same
Midmorning Snack: 1 glass of orange juice, lots of water
Mood After Snack: better

Mood Before Lunch: a little hungry
Time of Lunch: 12:00 pm
Lunch: light and dark meat chicken salad sandwich with mayonnaise, chopped celery and diced peppers, carrot sticks, orange juice and lots of water
Mood After Lunch: picking up some more

Mood Before Snack: ok
Midafternoon Snack: none - not hungry
Mood After Snack: ok

Mood Before Dinner: hungry, where the hell's Fran?
Time of Dinner: 6:30 pm
Dinner: rib steak, broccoli, boiled potato, tea
Mood After Dinner: ok, good meal

Mood Before Retiring: tired, Fran wants to "talk" to me, put her off till tomorrow, women and their diets - jeeze!
Time of Retiring: 11:00 pm

Paul H's Food/Mood Diary - Day 4

NAME: Paul H..   DATE: March 8, 2001
PHASE OF MENSTRUAL CYCLE:
__ MENSTRUAL   (DAYS 1- 4)
__ PREOVULATORY   (DAYS 5-14)
__ PREMENSTRUAL   (DAYS 15-28)
X NO CYCLE

Time at Arising: 6:30 am
Sleep Description: pretty good
Mood Upon Arising: ok, wanna play golf, skin condition
    still stinks, doc says it's all in my head, + I
    need to see a shrink . . . he's nuts!

Time of Breakfast: 7:00 am
Breakfast: 1/2 grapefruit, cup of oats with whole
    milk, decaf coffee (with whole milk)
Mood After Breakfast: ok, ready for golf

Mood Before Snack: getting hungry
Midmorning Snack: mixed nuts and raisins (ate on golf
    course)
Mood After Snack: better

Mood Before Lunch: not bad
Time of Lunch: 12:30 pm
Lunch: shrimp and mayonnaise with chopped celery in
    1/2 avocado, salad with spinach, cherry
    tomatoes, onions and broccoli, oil and lemon dressing
Mood After Lunch: ok, feel like doing something, don't
    wanna sit around and watch TV

Mood Before Snack: good
Midafternoon Snack: salted peanuts
Mood After Snack: good, feel like taking a walk

Mood Before Dinner: all right, skin still lousy
Time of Dinner: 6:30 pm
Dinner: chicken (breast and thigh), corn and Lima
   beans with pearl onions, cherry jello dessert, tea
Mood After Dinner: good, relaxed – talked to Fran, just
   listened, decided to keep my trap shut. I talk
   too much

Mood Before Retiring: ok, skin pretty bad but no
   worse than usual
Time of Retiring: 10:30 pm

The following diaries illustrate Paul's progress in the final phase of BioBalance Therapy, documenting his response to supplements appropriate for mixed metabolizers. These diaries summarize Paul's nutritional regimen for a 5-day period occurring approximately one month after he began taking supplements appropriate for him. This time frame has been selected to show you how his "stress related" skin condition was beginning to improve as well. Unlike Gloria, Paul did not experiment with supplements. It was clear to him that he was a mixed metabolizer, and would likely suffer an adverse reaction to the supplements appropriate for acid metabolizers.

Finally, note Paul's reactions on the days when he got sloppy and relied too heavily on foods appropriate for alkaline metabolizers. It's no surprise to see his hostility begin to re-emerge despite the fact that he was still taking supplements appropriate for mixed metabolizers on those days. Paul's attitude also illustrates the fact that human biochemistry has no memory. When you are in BioBalance, it's almost impossible to remember what it was like to be ill. Conversely, when you are out of BioBalance, it's all too easy to forget how well you felt when you were in BioBalance, and consequently it's easy blame everyone and everything around you for your state of disrepair, or "dis-ease"

Paul's Food/Mood Diaries With Supplements

Note: Paul tested his nutritional regimen for approximately one month without supplements before introducing the vitamins and minerals appropriate for his metabolic type.

Paul H's Food/Mood Diary - Day 1

NAME: Paul H..   DATE: May 2, 2001
PHASE OF MENSTRUAL CYCLE:
__ MENSTRUAL   (DAYS 1- 4)
__ PREOVULATORY   (DAYS 5-14)
__ PREMENSTRUAL   (DAYS 15-28)
X NO CYCLE

Time at Arising: 6:30 am
Sleep Description: good
Mood Upon Arising: good, skin is better, need a lot less
    cream to keep it clear

Time of Breakfast: 7:00 am
Breakfast: whole yogurt, peaches, mixed nut
    combination, decaf coffee with half and half
Mood After Breakfast: good, feel motivated - see if I
    can fix the car

Mood Before Snack: ok
Midmorning Snack: banana with peanut butter
Mood After Snack: good

Mood Before Lunch: a little hungry
Time of Lunch: 12:30 pm
Lunch: chili with meat (not too spicy)
Mood After Lunch: real good, kidding around with Fran,
    took a walk together

Mood Before Snack: good
Midafternoon Snack: none
Mood After Snack: still good

Mood Before Dinner: ok
Time of Dinner: 7:00 pm
Dinner: pan fried liver with onions, zucchini squash, brown rice with pat of butter
Mood After Dinner: feel fine, don't feel like watching TV, TV's a waste of time, took Fran out for a drive

Mood Before Retiring: sleepy
Time of Retiring: 10:30 pm

Paul H's Food/Mood Diary - Day 2

NAME: Paul H..   DATE: May 3, 2001
PHASE OF MENSTRUAL CYCLE:
__ MENSTRUAL   (DAYS 1- 4)
__ PREOVULATORY   (DAYS 5-14)
__ PREMENSTRUAL   (DAYS 15-28)
X NO CYCLE

Time at Arising: 6:00 am
Sleep Description: 7 1/2 hours deep sleep
Mood Upon Arising: relaxed

Time of Breakfast: 7:00 am
Breakfast: oat bran with whole milk, toast and peanut butter, decaf coffee
Mood After Breakfast: ready to get going

Mood Before Snack: ok
Midmorning Snack: not hungry – none
Mood After Snack: still good

Mood Before Lunch: getting hungry
Time of Lunch: 1:00 pm
Lunch: canned salmon with salad: spinach, cherry
  tomatoes, olives, sweet peppers, chopped onions,
  oil and vinegar dressing
Mood After Lunch: good, played 9 holes of golf

Mood Before Snack: good
Midafternoon Snack: mixed dried fruits and nuts on golf
  course
Mood After Snack: good

Mood Before Dinner: still good
Time of Dinner: 7:00 pm
Dinner: turkey broth, turkey thigh and breast
  meat, asparagus, carrots and white rice
Mood After Dinner: playful with Fran

Mood Before Retiring: really good, skin seems to be doing
  a lot better, haven't felt this well in a long
  time!
Time of Retiring: 10:00 pm

Paul H's Food/Mood Diary - Day 3

NAME: Paul H..   DATE: May 4, 2001
PHASE OF MENSTRUAL CYCLE:
__ MENSTRUAL   (DAYS 1- 4)
__ PREOVULATORY   (DAYS 5-14)
__ PREMENSTRUAL   (DAYS 15-28)
X NO CYCLE

Time at Arising: 6:00 am
Sleep Description: 8 hours, sound
Mood Upon Arising: good

Time of Breakfast: 6:45 am
Breakfast: coffee - no time to make breakfast, Fran's
    off visiting her relatives, had to play 18 holes
    of golf
Mood After Breakfast: good

Mood Before Snack: getting hungry
Midmorning Snack: 1 peach
Mood After Snack: weak and tired

Mood Before Lunch: still tired and impatient
Time of Lunch: 1:00 pm
Lunch: nothing much to eat - ate some leftover
    salad and a baked potato
Mood After Lunch: ok

Mood Before Snack: impatient
Midafternoon Snack: candy bar
Mood After Snack: why the hell does Fran have to
    go see her stupid relatives anyway. Gonna
    set her straight!

Mood Before Dinner: where the hell's the TV Guide, I suppose Fran took that too!!!

Time of Dinner: 8:00 pm

Dinner: cold cuts (chicken breast) with mustard on rye, 2 beers

Mood After Dinner: these vitamins are a rip off, they're not doin' a damn thing for me!!! It's Fran's fault for putting me on this dumb diet. First it was women and doctors, then it was women and their dumb notions about psychiatrists, and now it's women and their damn nutritionists!!! I'll show her when she gets back!

Mood Before Retiring: real angry

Time of Retiring: 12:00 am

Paul H's Food/Mood Diary - Day 4

NAME: Paul H..   DATE: May 5, 2001

PHASE OF MENSTRUAL CYCLE:

__ MENSTRUAL   (DAYS 1- 4)
__ PREOVULATORY   (DAYS 5-14)
__ PREMENSTRUAL   (DAYS 15-28)
X NO CYCLE

Time at Arising: 6:30 am

Sleep Description: not too hot

Mood Upon Arising: Gotta get hold of myself and get back on track, I was a real goof-off yesterday, what the hell's wrong with me?

Time of Breakfast: 7:00 am

Breakfast: hamburger patty, home fries, decaf coffee

Mood After Breakfast: *better than yesterday*

Mood Before Snack: *so-so, a little upset for no reason*
Midmorning Snack: *mixed nuts*
Mood After Snack: *ok*

Mood Before Lunch: *hungry, a little ticked*
Time of Lunch: *11:30 am*
Lunch: *canned dark meat tuna in oil,
    left over home fries*
Mood After Lunch: *better, almost normal*

Mood Before Snack: *good*
Midafternoon Snack: *peanut butter on whole wheat*
Mood After Snack: *still good*

Mood Before Dinner: *ok, gotta pick Fran up at airport*
Time of Dinner: *8:30 pm*
Dinner: *(ate out) pork chops, succotash with pat
    of butter, wild rice, small dish of vanilla ice
    cream*
Mood After Dinner: *much better, glad to see Fran again*

Mood Before Retiring: *ok*
Time of Retiring: *11:30 pm*

Paul H's Food/Mood Diary - Day 5

NAME: *Paul H..*   DATE: *May 6, 2001*
PHASE OF MENSTRUAL CYCLE:
__ MENSTRUAL   (DAYS 1- 4)
__ PREOVULATORY   (DAYS 5-14)
__ PREMENSTRUAL   (DAYS 15-28)
X NO CYCLE

Time at Arising: 7:00 am
Sleep Description: 7 1/2 hours, pretty good
Mood Upon Arising: went shopping for food,
 let Fran sleep late

Time of Breakfast: 10:00 am
Breakfast: oats with mixed nuts and seeds
 and whole yogurt
Mood After Breakfast: good

Mood Before Snack: ok
Midmorning Snack: none
Mood After Snack: still good

Mood Before Lunch: a little hungry
Time of Lunch: 2:00 pm
Lunch: sardine sandwich with mustard on rye,
 cup of split pea and onion soup
Mood After Lunch: real good

Mood Before Snack: still real good, took a walk alone,
 gave me a chance to think
Midafternoon Snack: none
Mood After Snack: still walking, walked 5 miles

Mood Before Dinner: good, noticed that
 my skin's lots better
Time of Dinner: 7:00 pm
Dinner: salmon steak with butter, white rice,
 corn niblets
Mood After Dinner: relaxed

Mood Before Retiring: relaxed, had a long talk with
 Fran, sorry I've been such a jerk, don't know
 how she's put up with me
Time of Retiring: 11:30 pm

The seven-day sample menu listed below will give you a concrete idea about how mixed metabolizers must eat in order to achieve and maintain a state of BioBalance. Once again, you may create your own menu provided you do so within the nutritional guidelines listed in the appendix.

Note that the regimen appropriate for mixed metabolizers bears a far stronger resemblance to the regimen appropriate for acid metabolizers than it does to the regimen appropriate for alkaline metabolizers. Also note that unlike acid metabolizers, mixed metabolizers need not always eat allowed or purine-rich meat, fish or poultry for breakfast. They must, however, always eat these foods for lunch and dinner.

Sample One Week Menu Appropriate for Mixed Types

Here's a sample of how a mixed type might eat during a seven-day period.

Day 1
Breakfast: Whole yogurt with fruit (especially apples, pears and bananas), mixed nuts and raw rolled oats; herbal tea (any variety). You may substitute "tofu" for whole yogurt. Tofu is a soy curd cake with custard-like consistency that is substantially alkaline-inducing in its potential (as might be expected since its primary ingredient is soy - a legume). Tofu may be purchased at many supermarkets and health food stores.
Lunch: New England clam chowder; light and dark meat tuna sandwich; dressing to consist of mayonnaise and chopped onion, celery and peppers on diet thin sliced bread, weak herbal tea (any variety).
Dinner: Prime rib, corn, broccoli, herbal tea (any variety).

Day 2
Breakfast: Cooked oats with whole milk or half and half, mixed nuts and seeds, herbal tea (any variety).
Lunch: Mild chili with beef, tossed salad with primary and secondary vegetables; olive oil and lemon dressing; herbal tea (any variety).
Dinner: Chicken (light and dark meat), asparagus tips and broccoli, brown rice; herbal tea (any variety).

Day 3
Breakfast: Sausage and egg(s) (eggs optional), fresh squeezed orange juice, diet thin sliced toast, herbal tea (any variety)

Lunch: Shrimp with mayonnaise and chopped onion, celery and bell peppers, stuffed in 1/2 an avocado, with tossed salad, herbal tea (any variety).

Dinner: Broiled salmon with drawn butter, brown rice, steamed broccoli, carrots, weak herbal tea (any variety), herbal tea (any variety).

Day 4
Breakfast: Bacon and egg(s) (eggs optional), grapefruit juice, herbal tea (any variety).

Lunch: Cream of broccoli soup, roast beef sandwich (any type of dressing), herbal tea (any variety).

Dinner: Stir fry with shrimp and scallops, brown rice, carrots, celery, cauliflower broccoli and onions, herbal tea (any variety).

Day 5
Breakfast: Corned beef hash and egg(s) (eggs optional), 1/2 grapefruit, diet thin sliced toast with butter, herbal tea (any variety).

Lunch: Chicken salad sandwich (light and dark meat), dressing to consist of mayonnaise and chopped celery, herbal tea (any variety).

Dinner: Pan fried liver (any variety) with onions, steamed cauliflower and broccoli, stir fried brown rice, herbal tea (any variety).

Day 6
Breakfast: Lamb patty and egg(s) (eggs optional); herbal tea (any variety).

Lunch: Tuna salad with chunk light tuna and white tuna, on leaf spinach, artichoke hearts, minced peppers and onions, assorted beans (waxed, Lima beans, string beans, etc.); dressing to consist of olive oil and small amount of fresh squeezed lemon (for flavor if desired), herbal tea (any variety).

Dinner: Pot roast, buttered corn on the cob, peas and carrots, herbal tea (any variety).

Day 7
Breakfast: Smoked salmon and egg(s), mixed fruit, herbal tea (any variety).
Lunch: Hamburger, tossed salad with assorted vegetables, herbal tea (any variety).
Dinner: Leg of lamb, spinach, zucchini, brown rice, herbal tea (any variety).

Once again, some mixed metabolizers do not respond well to a breakfast which includes purine-rich meats, fish or poultry, and do far better with lighter fare such as whole grain cereal, whole dairy, nuts, seed, etc.. Other mixed metabolizers find that their breakfast must include purine-rich meats, fish or poultry. In either case though, both lunch and dinner must include at least some purine-rich meat, fish or poultry as well as a mixture of primary and secondary vegetables.

The following are the most common mistakes made by mixed metabolizers

- **Avoiding meat, fish or poultry for lunch or dinner.** Some mixed metabolizers feel that they require meat, fish or poultry for breakfast as well.
- **Intermixing the primary and secondary foods unevenly over a series of meals.** For example, do not eat only primary foods with the primary meats, fish and poultry as the core of your meals for one or more days and then eat only the secondaries to compensate for this for several days. Eating in this fashion may indeed "balance out" over several days but your metabolic swings within that time frame will be severe and you will probably end up feeling awful.
- **Relying upon dairy and eggs as a substitute for primary and secondary meats, fish and poultry.** Recall, purine-rich foods form the basis or core of the regimen appropriate for mixed metabolizers. Dairy and eggs are purine deficient.

If possible, mixed metabolizers should use the appropriate premier regimen described in Chapter Two. Incidentally, given the fact that his wife did all of the cooking and that Paul was not interested in exploring the far-reaching implications of BioBalance Therapy, getting him to switch to the premier regimen was out of the question. However, his regular biocompatible regimen changed Paul's overall disposition. His wife was grateful for the change and it saved their marriage.

Chapter

7

Kimberly B. — A Cyclic Metabolizer:

In this chapter we will meet Kimberly B., a cyclic metabolizer. Before reviewing her situation let's review some basics. Remember that three basic principles of BioBalance Therapy were presented in Chapter One. The first of these needs to be restated here.

"There are three and only three static metabolic states. *At any point in time* every individual will be in one and only one of these three states. Therefore, *at any point in time* each individual can be classified as one and only one static metabolic type."

I purposely emphasize the words "*at any point in time.*" If you review these three principles, you will understand that:

- If you eat in a manner appropriate for your metabolic type, your psychological and physical well-being and performance will peak.
- If you inadvertently adopt a nutritional regimen that is completely inappropriate for your metabolic type, you will become extremely ill. That illness will probably manifest itself as a host of so-called "psychological", "psychogenic," "mental", "behavioral" or "stress-related" problems, but it may also manifest itself as one or more of a variety of physical problems.
- Finally, if you eat in a way that is neither optimally suited to your metabolic type nor completely inappropriate for your metabolic type, then your well-being and performance will suffer to varying degrees, and you will consequently experience suboptimal well-being. The matrix in Chapter One illustrates these three principles in picture format.

Thus far our case histories have profiled individuals whose metabolic types are static. That is to say, they are always either acid, alkaline or mixed. However, some individuals have a more complex BioProfile where their metabolic state changes from one type to another over time. These changes or transitions almost always occur predictably and in well-defined cyclic fashion. While cycling is not restricted to women, it occurs primarily with women who are premenopausal (still having menstrual cycles). Do not jump to the conclusion that all premenopausal women possess cyclic metabolic profiles. That's simply not the case. However, of the few people who are cyclers, most tend to be premenopausal women. These individuals typically report that they are relatively symptom-free during one part of their menstrual cycle but that they suffer a host of symptoms during the remainder of their cycle.

These symptoms are the result of an intermediary metabolic imbalance. It should be logical that a cyclic metabolizer will respond favorably to a nutritional regimen during one phase of her cycle, and then respond unfavorably to that very same regimen during another phase of her cycle. Theoretically, the metabolic state a cycler occupies can vary based upon the time of day, month or year. But with few exceptions, cyclers are premenopausal women cycling within a monthly (i.e., 28 day) pattern.

Now let's look at Kimberly B. as an example of a metabolic cycler. She is 42 years old and reports suffering from premenstrual syndrome or PMS. She generally eats "light" because she is weight conscious and fears that added fats would cause her to gain weight. She avoids red meats because she fears that red meats will also make her fat and place her at high risk for cardiovascular disease. She avoids legumes (peas and beans) because she reports that they give her gas.

Kimberly typically felt reasonably well until the 14th day of her cycle, when she ovulated. At that time her symptoms emerged, and remained with her until the end of day 28 when her period began. The symptoms included extreme breast tenderness, bloating, irritability, fatigue, depression, free-floating anxiety, night sweats, panic awakenings, hot flashes, nausea, dizziness, insomnia and erratic mood swings.

Since Kimberly generally ate "light" and felt well from day 1 through 14, she was probably metabolizing in an alkaline mode during that time. Furthermore, given that she became highly symptomatic from day 15 through day 28 on the same "light" regimen, it was likely that she became nonalkaline (either acid or mixed) during the premenstrual phase of her cycle. Very significantly, Kimberly found she was caffeine tolerant during her menstrual and pre-ovulatory phases, and caffeine intolerant during her premenstrual phase. A noticeable switch of caffeine tolerance like this almost always indicates a transition from an alkaline state to a nonalkaline state.

The diaries below summarize Kimberly's reactions to her initial acid-inducing challenge meals on day 14 of her menstrual cycle. Her poor psychophysiological state on the morning of day 15 of her cycle immediately suggested to her that her metabolic status must have transitioned on the night of her 14th cycle day when she likely ovulated. Most women can usual tell within several hours, if and when their metabolisms transition. Consequently, Kimberly's observations are not at all unusual. Kimberly's observations show that she was indeed a metabolic cycler. She transitioned from an alkaline state which lasted from day 1 through 14, to a nonalkaline state which lasted from day 15 through 28.

Kimberly's Food/Mood Diaries for challenge meals taken on the 14th and 15th day of her cycle (without supplements) are shown below. Once again, note that Kimberly responds well to the "light" (alkaline-appropriate or acid-inducing) diet when she is alkaline on cycle day #14 (representative of her response during cycles days 1 through 14). Conversely, during the night of cycle day 14 and on the morning of cycle day 15 Kimberly reports feeling poorly, suggesting that she has transitioned from an alkaline to a nonalkaline state at the end of cycle day 14 (ovulation). Consequently, on the morning of her 15th cycle day, she takes appropriate nutritional countermeasures by adhering to the "heavy" regimen appropriate for nonalkaline types.

Kimberly's Food/Mood Diaries for Challenge Meals at Midcycle

DAY 1 (Cycle Day #14 - Preovulatory Phase)

NAME: Kimberly B.   DATE: February 10, 2001
PHASE OF MENSTRUAL CYCLE:
__ MENSTRUAL   (DAYS 1- 4)
X PREOVULATORY   (DAYS 5-14)
__ PREMENSTRUAL   (DAYS 15-28)
14 DAY NUMBER IN CYCLE
__ NO CYCLE

Time of Breakfast: 7:00 am
Breakfast: strong black coffee with sugar and skim milk, 1 orange, 1 rice cake
Mood After Breakfast: cheerful, motivated, ready to go

Mood Before Snack: great, upbeat
Midmorning Snack: none
Mood After Snack: still going strong

Mood Before Lunch: good
Time of Lunch: 12:30 pm
Lunch: 1% fat yogurt with fruit - tangerine slices, apple slices, melon, pineapple chunks, cherries, coffee
Mood After Lunch: great, cheerful, extroverted, focused, feeling fine

---

Mood Before Snack: still going strong
Midafternoon Snack: none
Mood After Snack: feel fine

Mood Before Dinner: good
Time of Dinner: 7:00 pm
Dinner: baked scrod with fresh squeezed lemon, broccoli, brown rice, herbal tea

Mood After Dinner: somewhat tired

Mood Before Retiring: beat, ULTRA-tired. Something's wrong, I'm not feeling as well as I felt throughout the day. Curiously, this is the time of month when I typically ovulate. Perhaps I'm transitioning from alkaline to nonalkaline. I'll see what happens tomorrow.

Time of Retiring: 10:00 pm

DAY 2 (Cycle Day #15 - Probably Ovulating - Entering Premenstrual Phase)

NAME: Kimberly B.   DATE: February 11, 2001

PHASE OF MENSTRUAL CYCLE:

__ MENSTRUAL   (DAYS 1- 4)

X PREOVULATORY   (DAYS 5-14)

__ PREMENSTRUAL   (DAYS 15-28)

15 DAY NUMBER IN CYCLE

__ NO CYCLE

Time at Arising: 7:00 am

Sleep Description: AWFUL. 9 hours, had 2 panic awakenings, bed sheets soaked with perspiration

Mood Upon Arising: HORRIBLE. bloated, dizzy, feel like I've got a hangover. That's pretty typical for how my PMS starts. Lousy, irritable, tender breasts, nauseous, depressed. Wish I were a man so I wouldn't have to put up with this! I've responded really well to the "light" diet during my entire menstrual and pre-ovulatory phases (days 1 through 4, and days 5 through 14 respectively), and now I'm responding poorly to that same diet on the day of ovulation. I think I'm cycling. I'll try switching diets to the "heavy" regimen, and fine-tune it later.

Time of Breakfast: 7:00 am
Breakfast: smoked kippers (herrings) and fried egg, 1 slice
    well-buttered toast, weak decaf herbal tea
Mood After Breakfast: somewhat better but not great

Mood Before Snack: ok, but just ok, and
    running down a bit
Midmorning Snack: rice cake with lots of almond
    butter and weak herbal tea
Mood After Snack: picked up a bit

Mood Before Lunch: running down again
Time of Lunch: 11:30 am
Lunch: bean with bacon soup, bacon cheeseburger
    (ate out), cup of decaf tea.
Mood After Lunch: better again

Mood Before Snack: ok
Midafternoon Snack: peanuts
Mood After Snack: picked up again

Mood Before Dinner: running down somewhat, tired,
    cold and achy. the usual PMS symptoms.
Time of Dinner: 6:00 pm
Dinner: pan fried chicken liver in butter with bacon
    and mushrooms, fried cauliflower, green beans,
    weak herbal tea
Mood After Dinner: much better

Mood Before Retiring: not great, but TONS better
    than this time last month
Time of Retiring: 10:00 pm

Kimberly knew she was nonalkaline during her premenstrual phase. Her next concern was to determine whether she was acid or mixed during this time. A little trial-and-error with her dietary regimens enabled Kimberly to determine that she transitioned to an acid mode and not a mixed mode on the night of her 14th-to-15th cycle day. Her rationale for this conclusion stemmed primarily from the fact that her reactions to the alkaline-appropriate regimen (the light regimen) were extremely severe when she became premenstrual on cycle day 15, and that she improved dramatically by excluding virtually all foods appropriate for alkaline metabolizers starting on cycle day number 15.

The next set of diaries tracks Kimberly on days 14 through 15 of her next menstrual cycle. This time around, Kimberly adhered to the nutritional regimen appropriate for alkaline metabolizers (the light regimen) plus taking the companion supplements for alkaline metabolizers during her menstrual and preovulatory phases only (cycle days 1 through 4, and cycle days 5 through 14 respectively). Anticipating a negative reaction to the regimen appropriate for alkaline metabolizers after dinner of cycle day #14, Kimberly switched to the regimen appropriate for acid metabolizers for dinner on cycle day #14. She thereby successfully avoided the adverse reaction to the light dinner she had eaten the preceding month.

Kimberly's Food/Mood Diaries at Midcycle With Supplements

DAY 1 (Cycle Day #14 - Preovulatory Phase)

NAME: Kimberly B.   DATE: March 10, 2001
PHASE OF MENSTRUAL CYCLE:
__ MENSTRUAL   (DAYS 1- 4)
X PREOVULATORY   (DAYS 5-14)
__ PREMENSTRUAL   (DAYS 15-28)
14 DAY NUMBER IN CYCLE
__ NO CYCLE

Time at Arising: *8:00 am*
Sleep Description: *7 hours, good*
Mood Upon Arising: *Good*

Time of Breakfast: *7:00 am*
Breakfast: *strong black coffee with sugar and skim milk, 1 orange, 1 rice cake + alkaline-appropriate supplements*
Mood After Breakfast: *fine, ready to get going*

Mood Before Snack: *up beat*
Midmorning Snack: *none*
Mood After Snack: *still going strong*

Mood Before Lunch: *good*
Time of Lunch: *1:30 pm*
Lunch: *1% fat yogurt with fruit - tangerine slices, apple slices, melon, pineapple chunks, cherries, coffee + alkaline-appropriate supplements*
Mood After Lunch: *feeling fine*

Mood Before Snack: *excellent*
Midafternoon Snack: *none*
Mood After Snack: *still feel good*

Mood Before Dinner: *good*
Time of Dinner: *7:00 pm*
Dinner: *broiled salmon steak, with stir-fried cauliflower, peas, and mushrooms + baked potato with sour cream and butter, weak herbal decaf tea + acid-appropriate supplements*
Mood After Dinner: *still pretty good*

Mood Before Retiring: *still good. tired in a "normal" way*
Time of Retiring: *11:00 pm*

DAY 2 (Cycle Day #15 - Premenstrual Phase)

NAME: Kimberly B.   DATE: March 11, 2001
PHASE OF MENSTRUAL CYCLE:
__ MENSTRUAL   (DAYS 1- 4)
__ PREOVULATORY   (DAYS 5-14)
X PREMENSTRUAL   (DAYS 15-28)
15 DAY NUMBER IN CYCLE
__ NO CYCLE

Time at Arising: 6:00 am
Sleep Description: 7 hours, deep sleep. No panic
    awakenings!
Mood Upon Arising: rested, focused, ready to go, and
    RAVENOUSLY hungry.

Breakfast: bacon and eggs with fried potatoes,
    decaf coffee with heavy cream + acid-
    appropriate supplements
Mood After Breakfast: not hungry, still feel reasonably well

Mood Before Snack: good, took a walk
Midmorning Snack: mixed nuts
Mood After Snack: still good

Mood Before Lunch: a little tired
Time of Lunch: 12:30 am
Lunch: dark meat tuna (canned) packed in olive oil,
    hard boiled egg with mayonnaise ("egg boat"),
    1 1/2 slices of Ezekial bread + acid-appropriate
    supplements.
Mood After Lunch: lots better

Mood Before Snack: "up"
Midafternoon Snack: rice cake with thick
    slab of almond butter

Mood After Snack: good

Mood Before Dinner: running down a little
Time of Dinner: 7:00 pm
Dinner: pan-fried steak, stir-fried peas and carrots
   with wild rice, decaf tea, + acid-appropriate
   supplements
Mood After Dinner: really good

Mood Before Retiring: relaxed and sleepy
Time of Retiring: 10:30 pm

A final note. It would be a mistake to think that Kimberly's BioProfile is THE metabolic profile for ALL women who suffer PMS. Recall that *individuals possess BioProfiles; disorders do not.* Consequently, there are as many BioProfiles for PMS as there are women who suffer from it. Although, most women who suffer some type of menstrual disorder (whether *pre*menstrual, *post*menstrual, menstrual, or any combination thereof) typically switch from one of the three possible static metabolic states to one and only one other. Consequently, most cyclers are *bipolar* metabolizers. While *tripolar* metabolizers exist, they are extremely rare. I would urge you to abide by the following guidelines in determining your BioProfile:

- Do not automatically conclude that if your symptoms cycle, then your metabolic state must switch as well.
- Do not make your BioProfile more complicated than it likely is.
- Let the caffeine tolerance test be your primary guide in determining your BioProfile.

Therefore, if you are a woman suffering from PMS let the caffeine tolerance test be your primary guide in determining whether you are cyclic. Track your ups and downs via a set of food-mood diaries as Kimberly did over a period of two complete menstrual cycles (the first without supplements, and the second with supplements).

Chapter

8

Conclusion

In this sequel to my first book, I have given you a powerful tool. That tool consists of a simplified, non-technical how-to/hands-on guide for the application of BioBalance Therapy. Using the caffeine tolerance test, you can now quickly and easily determine your BioProfile without blood tests, and at virtually no expense. I have also provided you with three new and improved nutritional regimens for the three static metabolic types. These three new regimens are in addition to the regimens in my first book, and they are better for two important reasons:

- They enhance BioBalance Therapy's previous success rate. Specifically, they allow you to achieve BioBalance while simultaneously minimizing the possibility of unwanted side effects such as candidiasis (systemic yeast infections), allergic reactions and gastro-intestinal upset.
- They have far fewer undesirable environmental impacts than the original three nutritional regimens.

In effect, we now have a "new and improved" BioBalance methodology. While I remain ever more certain of the efficacy of this program, it does strike at the very heart of long-held traditions within the medical and psychiatric professions. The implications and repercussions of BioBalance are profound and far-reaching. They are worth summarizing again, hence this final chapter.

BioBalance is a testable procedure. Not only can patients be tested to measure their pH levels, but the results of implementing BioBalance Therapy can also be tested for its effectiveness. As stated earlier, BioBalance Therapy has shown itself to be almost universally effective, producing positive results in 75-80% of cases. BioBalance is built on relatively simple concepts:

A. Every individual has his/her own BioProfile, or in other words, his/her own ideal metabolic tendency and pH level.
B. When an individual strays from his/her ideal pH level—typically through nutritional intake—the function of various systems of the body, including the brain and central nervous system, are compromised.
C. Symptoms of this non-ideal pH condition can range over a broad spectrum, but frequently include so-called psychological disorders that are almost impossible to diagnose correctly without knowledge of BioBalance Therapy. These include anxiety, depression, chronic fatigue, panic attacks, insomnia, PMS, chronic headaches, digestive disorders, weight problems, bloating, inability to concentrate, and a host of other conditions often felt to be induced by psychological stress.
D. Because conventional medicine does not screen for blood pH, nor does it attempt to alter blood pH, but rather focuses on treating symptoms, patients with pH imbalances often find no relief from any traditional treatment and end up in a never-ending cycle of new and different medicines until their doctors conclude the problems are all psychological, since no treatments yield positive results.
E. BioBalance proposes that the cause of many of these problems is, in fact, pH imbalance and offers non-invasive, nutritional means to adjust pH so the symptoms will disappear. Since pH is not routinely considered in diagnosing patients, many treatment plans are incorrect, sometimes actually aggravating an existing problem simply because it makes pH imbalance worse.

As simple as these concepts are, it is almost impossible to be neutral on BioBalance Therapy. These concepts call into question much of the medical and psychotherapeutic work being done in the world today. I feel it would be irresponsible of me if I neglected pointing out these implications.

In my first book I discussed the poor measures of effectiveness of psychotherapy in detail. In so doing I discussed why psychotherapy in its many forms and disguises is inadequate and inappropriate for treating many disorders commonly and erroneously classified as "mental," "psychological," "psychogenic," or (as is now more fashionable) "stress-induced," or "stress-related."

I am convinced that many of these disorders are *iatrogenic,* or physician-induced. Why? Because for reasons which should now be clear to you, these disorders have been created and/or aggravated by the attending physician through his/her misdiagnosis, mislabeling and subsequent inappropriate treatment.

It is *not* true that the percentage of these problems that are misdiagnosed by primary health care practitioners is small. Statistics suggest that as many as 75% of patients seeking assistance through primary health care are misdiagnosed in this fashion, and the majority of them end up on what I call the "administrative trash heap" of medicine, namely psychotherapeutic care. Tragically, most of these patients are women.

In my critique of psychotherapy in my first book, I explained that all schools of psychotherapeutic thought tacitly assume that emotional distress is solely *learned* or *socially programmed* via interactive verbal and/or nonverbal cues. Consequently, psychotherapy seeks to find a cure for the problem through the same means; it tries to bring relief of emotional distress through some form of verbal or social interaction, by "talking things over," more commonly known as "the talking cure." In other words, since it is assumed that you have been programmed by some combination of social and verbal/nonverbal cues to be anxious or depressed or to suffer PMS or chronic fatigue, etc., then it is concluded that effective treatment may be brought about by de-programming you using similar types of cues, by "talking things over/acting things out," or more generally, "emoting" with some guidance from a trained counselor or practitioner. My experience in researching and applying BioBalance Therapy has convinced me beyond question that this assumption and its conclusion are in all likelihood incorrect. I have encountered no evidence since writing my first book to suggest that my views on this point are unrealistic or too extreme.

In saying this, I do not want to suggest that humans are nothing more than walking-talking metabolisms whose behaviors are uniquely driven by the foods they eat. On the contrary, I believe a reductionist approach is doomed to failure. What is reductionism? Reductionism proposes that human behavior in its entirety can be understood solely in terms of molecular interactions. Nevertheless, I must emphasize that my conclusions regarding psychotherapy's ineffectiveness are not generalizations based upon the actions of a few abusive and incompetent practitioners. I can say that psychotherapy is ineffective for many of the disorders mentioned in this book, because repeated statistical research has shown it to be no more effective in treating them than placebo therapy.

What is a placebo? It is a chemically neutral 'pill,' usually water or glycerin, that is known to have no chemical/organic/physiological effect on the body. The only reason a placebo can have a positive effect is psychological, i.e. the patient thinks he/she is receiving a real and beneficial drug, and that faith alone ultimately yields the positive effect. Placebo effect is real. It manifests itself in a small percentage of cases. *But before any therapy can be considered effective, it must produce positive results more frequently than a placebo does.*

The Food and Drug Administration routinely requires placebo testing to determine whether a particular drug proposed by a pharmaceutical company is more effective than a water pill, i.e. does it have a measurable effectiveness that goes beyond the mere power of suggestion in treating a specific disorder? If not, the drug is denied approval by the FDA. A similar formal standard is applied in evaluating surgical techniques.

I believe such a standard should be applied in determining the efficacy of psychotherapy. Specifically, we must objectively try to determine if psychotherapy is any more effective than a placebo. How do you create a placebo in psychotherapy? By having an untrained imposter masquerade as a psychotherapist and go through the motions of administering psychotherapy. If, under these conditions, the "placebo treatment" produces results as good as or better than those produced by a trained psychotherapist, we have a case for saying that psychotherapy is a hoax—at least as it pertains to the disorders often caused by pH imbalance. Tests of this nature are not difficult to apply, and their application does not require a deep understanding of how the human mind or psyche operates.

In fact, this whole idea of actually testing psychotherapy's effectiveness is not a new one. In the early 1980's a team of researchers at the University of Connecticut set out to do just that. (See Prioleau, et al, in the references at the back of this book.) They found no solid evidence that psychotherapy is any more effective than placebo treatment. If you take the time to read this study, you will find that it is, in fact, a compilation of numerous studies which includes thousands of patient-practitioner contact hours, over a broad spectrum of different emotional disorders and so-called "schools of psychotherapeutic thought." This type of compilation, called *meta-analysis,* is widely used in avoiding costly and time-consuming duplication of research. The results of this meta-analysis are so exhaustive and so compelling that its authors concluded that hundreds of additional studies would have to contradict their evidence in order to reverse the negative trend documented up to that point in time. In fact, it has been suggested that in some cases, placebo psychotherapy has outperformed psychotherapy.

That's how abysmally poor psychotherapy's track record is. In plain English, ***psychotherapy has <u>repeatedly</u> failed*** to prove itself to be superior to its water pill/placebo comparison test. The Prioleau study was the equivalent of a nuclear explosion in the world of psychotherapy. The researchers became pariahs instead of recognized for their diligence. The study is rarely quoted today, despite the tremendous work that went into it.

If you read the prologue to this book, you'll see how hostile and vicious the academic and professional psychotherapeutic priesthood becomes when the sanctity of their "talking cure" is questioned. This is especially tragic when you consider the history of psychotherapy. Before psychotherapy came into its own, individuals who suffered from emotional disorders were treated like objects of amusement, warehoused in filth-ridden institutions, and abused, tortured or killed as witches and agents of the devil. At the dawn of the age of enlightenment, courageous social reformers realized that emotionally distressed individuals required humane treatment. These reformers changed our social institutions for the better. It's a shame to see that the intellectual heirs of these reformers have turned what was once a noble endeavor into a cultural/political power struggle, apparently for ego and money.

Unfortunately, the psychotherapeutic lobby has now become so powerful that it has arm-twisted the FDA into waiving the all-important placebo standard in evaluating the effectiveness of psychotherapy. In other words, the FDA has allowed for a double standard: a stringent standard that applies to all scientific disciplines; and a meaningless nonstandard which psychotherapy applies to itself!

Yes, it is true that some individuals do report feeling temporarily better *after* receiving psychotherapy. What does that prove? In light of the evidence, any intelligent person has to ask if this improvement materialized *in spite of* psychotherapeutic treatment, rather than *because of* it. If we persist in believing the latter, then we have committed ourselves to believing in magic and superstition. At the very least we are trying to have faith in a therapy that statistically works no better than null therapy (no therapy at all).

Incidentally, historically it has been common practice for the pseudo-sciences such as psychotherapy to use the language of the established sciences in an attempt to look credible to the public and gain an aura of legitimacy. Special and general relativity, quantum physics, information theory, chaos theory, thermodynamics, electrodynamics, and statistical mechanics were and are among the disciplines within the natural sciences whose vocabulary is repeatedly raided by the pseudosciences. Currently, New Age occultism (in addition to psychotherapy) is famous for these forays. In this fashion, a modern day appeal to magic is being used to frighten people who have been successfully treated for emotional distress with psychopharmaceuticals (medications) into endless psychotherapeutic treatment. This is not curing anything. Many psychotherapists are telling their patients that if they do not continue to receive psychotherapy, then their illness will return despite their medication.

Analogously, imagine if I succeeded in convincing you that the sun rises daily because I make it do so each morning. Worse yet, imagine if I frightened you into paying me a handsome fee to make the sun rise each day. If ongoing psychotherapy could demonstrate that it could prevent emotional distress from returning after successful treatment with the talking cure, then psychotherapy would have beaten out its placebo competitor with flying colors. ***But it has not.*** Consequently, any intelligent person has to conclude that scare tactics such as these are born out of ignorance, cruelty or greed. I know this statement sounds incredible, especially in the wake of decades of professional and mass media propoganda regarding the treatment of emotional distresses. But the facts stand on their own. It is time we paid attention to them.

Some individuals will always believe that psychotherapy is effective despite evidence to the contrary. I call these people *true believers*. Sadly, branches of academia, popular culture and the media have done little to disabuse people of this mistaken belief, and have in fact gone out of their way to fortify it.

In my first book, through several case histories, I illustrated the extent to which some true believers will go in tenaciously clinging to the notion that psychotherapy is effective. Typically, these individuals are either psychotherapists or patients who understandably don't wish to be told that their intellectual, emotional and financial investments have been wasted. Their plight is analogous to the plight of the emperor in the fable *The Emperor's New Clothes*. In this children's story, a clever tailor dupes the emperor into believing that he (the tailor) has created a splendid imperial wardrobe, when in fact no clothes have been created. The gullible emperor is so badly hoodwinked, that he parades stark naked through his empire's capital city. The emperor's fawning courtiers wish at all expense to deny the truth and withhold it from him. Only innocent and "uneducated" children openly acknowledged the scam.

Many patients suffering from severe and chronic emotional distress also feel that their pain is somehow trivialized if they are told that a prime cause of their distress results from how they eat—a "mere metabolic imbalance" which may be corrected by something as mundane and trivial as proper acid/alkaline nutrition. I can't tell you the number of times I have heard the following from a reluctant candidate for BioBalance Therapy: "Well, I'm sure that nutrition is okay for some people, but my problems are far too complex for something as simple as BioBalance Therapy." For these reasons, people suffering from emotional distress are among the most difficult to treat. Paradoxically, (and with more than a little help from the psychotherapeutic community), these people have become addicted to what I call the "let's talk about me" syndrome - a version of the "talking cure" that subtly reinforces ego needs, without addressing the underlying physical causes of emotional distress. All this despite the fact that years of talking things over with sensitive experts has done little if anything to improve their lot.

Such reactions are understandable since many of psychotherapy's victims are people who are desperately searching for meaning in their suffering, and psychotherapy has exploited their pain by implying that the talking cure will somehow shed light on that meaning—given enough time and enough money, of course. Furthermore, and of equal importance, emotional distress subtly and insidiously strikes at an individual's very core, thus threatening the victim's sanity and causing the victim to question his/her own *existence*.

(If you've never suffered chronic and deep-seated emotional distress, you may self-induce this type of distress by eating in bio-*in*compatible fashion for several days, although I don't recommend it. Individuals who believe that the emotionally disturbed experience emotions like the rest of us, but simply behave in a different fashion, should take me up on this challenge.)

Ironically then, for the reasons listed above, BioBalance Therapy sometimes meets with opposition from those very individuals who stand to benefit most from it. Consequently, BioBalance Therapy is at once both liberating and confining. It is liberating since it can end the anguish of chronic emotional distress. It is confining since that liberation is not brought about through the discovery of any profound and pivotal "personal insights" unless of course you define knowledge of the metabolic bridge between mind and body as a pivotal insight. At any rate, as much of an insight as it may be, a metabolic insight can hardly be classified as personal, and is thus viewed as irrelevant to someone in the throes of emotional distress.

To quote the philosopher and historian Will Durant, "Knowledge narrows hope." This seems to describe the evolutionary path of all scientific progress. The tension between the cold austere beauty of the hard or natural sciences, and the warm passion of the arts and humanities will always lie at the root of the so-called "war between the cultures," (the sciences versus the humanities). BioBalance is not exempt from this tension. It is unfortunate that people committed to an artistic view of life often view the triumph of BioBalance as a defeat of humanism. I feel that this view is unnecessarily restrictive but understandable. If these people would only pause and understand that science's progress in the realm of the emotions (historically the inner sanctum of the humanities) is not a victory for reductionism, then perhaps they wouldn't take such a hard line in defending a failed therapy (psychotherapy), causing them in turn to repudiate so powerful a tool as BioBalance Therapy.

Unfortunately, psychotherapy's stranglehold continues to be subsidized by insurance companies and by the federal government. But it appears that the extent of this support has lessened since psychotherapy's heyday in the

United States during the period extending from the 1950s through the early 1980s. Evidently, even insurance companies are beginning to realize that psychotherapy's effectiveness is at best severely limited. Has there been any insurance coverage for BioBalance Therapy? Of course not. Given the historical precedent for breakthroughs in medicine, and the treatment of disease in general, it's my guess that it will take quite some time before the insurance/private sector, the government, and the medical profession wake up to this oversight. Then again, by making it so easy for individuals to implement BioBalance Therapy on their own, I have minimized the need for insurance coverage of its application. In a way this is good, since I fear that if BioBalance were driven by a complex set of laws, then it too might spin off yet another priesthood, jealous of its turf, and fanatical in its attempt to thwart the next major revolution in the solution of an even more complex food-mood-health puzzle. As is the case with science, progress and proof must result from the application of reason, and not by proclamation from authority (i.e., the multi-certified sensitivity experts).

What are the practical implications of all this? I feel that they are two-fold:

- You don't need insurance coverage to undergo BioBalance Therapy, since a reasonable test for determining your BioProfile is available at little or no cost. Anyone can take the caffeine tolerance test. In the final analysis, you are fully empowered to implement BioBalance Therapy. As Dr. Jack Woodard, M.D. states in the foreword to this book, one way or another you have to eat, so why not eat in biocompatible fashion? You don't really need an M.D., an insurance company or a federal bureaucracy to watch over you and give you its approval, although I am legally compelled to tell you that you shouldn't pursue any type of nutritional treatment on your own without medical supervision.

- As far as psychotherapy is concerned, nothing would be gained by attempting to stop the practice of an ineffective therapy (the talking cure) providing we are sure the therapy does no harm. If some people feel they simply must talk things over with sensitive experts, albeit for a fee, they should be entitled to do so. However, I also feel that psychotherapy—absent the administration of pharmaceuticals—

should be deregulated. Market forces should ultimately decide hourly talker/listener fees. After all, if you knew that psychotherapy was no more effective than placebo therapy, but felt nonetheless that you simply had to talk things over with a professional talker/listener, then you and (s)he should determine the financial worth of that transaction with as little government interference as possible. In this vein, anyone who wants to advertise him/herself as a professional talker/listener should be entitled to do so.

• Once again, to insure public safety I feel that dispensation of prescription drugs must be conducted under the oversight of an impartial professional agency. In the event the psychotherapist becomes abusive and engages in misconduct, then these instances need to be tried in a court of law on a case-by-case basis. Otherwise, there is really little if any need to regulate dialogue/verbal transactions between or among two or more consenting adults. If deregulation of the psychotherapeutic profession were pursued, fees would certainly tumble, and psychotherapy would become affordable to anyone who seeks it out. Indeed, as the public became more informed, I would further wager that psychotherapy, as we now know it, would ultimately wither away.

Does this mean that a viable verbal alternative to BioBalance Therapy will never be found? Never is a long time. In the ultimate scheme of things my answer to this question would have to be: I don't know. If practitioners within the psychotherapeutic community were intellectually honest and ethical, they too would state that they didn't know, instead of trying to pass themselves off as uniquely expert in the field of the human mind/psyche.

Since the problem of finding an effective model of verbal or social intervention has not yet been satisfactorily developed, this area should legitimately remain open to research. But in any event, ineffective talking therapies should not be passed off onto a gullible and vulnerable public as being effective. Once again, I state that they are ineffective because they have failed to pass placebo trials. I cannot say with certainty why they are ineffective, but that is not the issue. I can only say that research shows that they are ineffective.

It is important to be clear on this point. The ineffectiveness of psychotherapy is not a matter of opinion; it is a researched fact. Conversely, the effectiveness of BioBalance Therapy and the relative effectiveness of other nutritional therapies is also not my point of view or my opinion. It is a fact. Indeed, if the purveyors of nutritional therapy today subjected their so-called cures to the same rigor to which BioBalance Therapy has been subjected, they would see how limited their success rates are, and they would not try to pass their therapies off as anything more than partial remedies serving one sub-spectrum of a broader metabolic spectrum, namely "the acid/alkaline elephant" (see Chapter One)—a huge reality whose very existence is daily overlooked by the medical and psychotherapeutic communities.

A similar though less incriminating critique may be directed at the holistic, alternative or complementary health care community. While holistic medicine's techniques are not as ineffective as psychotherapy's, they are rarely more effective than the many nutritional therapies outside of BioBalance Therapy being hawked in today's "mass market." I've already summarized those success rates in tabular form in Chapter One of this book.

Does all of this mean that BioBalance Therapy is the "silver bullet" being sought by the holistic medical community? No, of course not, but it does mean that good medical practice desperately requires a standard procedure, a *critical path* consisting of an initial pH screening, to correctly diagnose and treat disease. Once again, in plain English, determining the patient's acid/alkaline metabolic type or BioProfile should be the very first thing the physician does in making a diagnosis or assessing an appropriate treatment plan. If such an initial screening were routine medical practice, most health care providers would discover that in many cases—once the patient's BioProfile is correctly determined and once BioBalance therapy is appropriately applied—additional significant medical care would not be required.

Yes, of course there will be cases where additional health care will be required, such as treatment for candidiasis, or the Epstein-Barr virus or whatever else seems to be compounding the problem. Unfortunately, by failing to institute a critical path with an initial pH screening test, the practitioner is figuratively placing the cart before the horse, and is tying up far too many patients in an endless series of unnecessary treatments. In essence, *BioBalance Therapy is always necessary in treating the individual, and in many cases, BioBalance Therapy is both necessary and sufficient.*

How can I make this statement with such confidence? Because my research consistently shows that the correlation between the type of disorders to which I refer in this book on the one hand, and acid/alkaline metabolic imbalance on the other, is extremely strong. The correlation connecting these same disorders to other factors currently being hawked as "missing diagnoses" by the medical community, is not nearly as strong. In fact, in many cases where the patient is suffering from an acid/alkaline imbalance in addition to (for example) a yeast overgrowth (candidiasis), or the Epstein-Barr virus, simply eliminating the underlying imbalance is enough to achieve remission of symptoms. Why? Because there are more than a few perfectly healthy individuals who harbor a yeast overgrowth and/or the Epstein-Barr virus, but virtually no healthy individuals who possess a significant and unchecked intermediary metabolic imbalance.

A Final Word on Hypoglycemia and Diabetes

Perhaps the single most misunderstood, misdiagnosed and mistreated disorder encountered by the health care community is hypoglycemia. I single out hypoglycemia in this final commentary because it illustrates the chaos in both holistic and allopathic medicine in treating patients without employing the *critical path*—the initial pH screen—to which I have referred.

The word hypoglycemia has as its roots the Greek words *hypo* and *glycemia*, meaning "low" and "sugar" respectively. Consequently, if you are a true hypoglycemic, you suffer from low blood sugar. There is only one way you can suffer from low blood sugar, and that is if you metabolize blood sugar too rapidly. If you have ever studied biochemistry and metabolic rate kinetics, you know that virtually all hypoglycemics also possess chronically low venous plasma pH levels. Conversely, virtually all individuals who suffer from chronically low venous plasma pH levels are also hypoglycemic. In other words, true hypoglycemics *by definition* possess nonalkaline metabolic profiles (i.e., they are either acid or mixed metabolizers depending upon the severity of their hypoglycemia.) Conversely, it is impossible for a hypoglycemic patient to possess an alkaline imbalance. There are two foolproof ways to determine if you are hypoglycemic, and they involve a test of your venous plasma pH or your caffeine tolerance. The latter is, of course, far easier to apply.

What about Glucose Tolerance Tests? I cannot emphasize too strongly that the multi-hour Glucose Tolerance Test, and the hypoglycemia symptom test are often worthless since they tell you nothing about your underlying metabolic imbalance. Consequently, if your health care provider has diagnosed you as being hypoglycemic based upon the fact that your glucose tolerance curve looked erratic or because you had "classic symptoms," you may have likely been sold a bill of goods.

I cannot tell you the number of refugees of both allopathic and holistic medicine I've treated, who have been unwittingly duped into believing that they were hypoglycemic by well-intentioned practitioners when, in fact, they were not. Conversely, I cannot tell you the number of true hypoglycemics who were incorrectly treated for some other problem, also by well-intentioned health care practitioners. Sadly, many of these individuals went on to become presidents in local chapters of various hypoglycemia societies created to help others, based on their own personal experiences. In this way, massive amounts of misinformation have unwittingly been promulgated throughout a community desperately seeking relief from a very real disturbance.

If you track the various treatments for hypoglycemia over the past 30 years you will note that the holistic community has been comedic in its 180° dietary reversals, and about-face-, forward march-, backward march-, side-ways crab march hypoglycemia treatment plans. In the 1970s the established treatment for hypoglycemia consisted of high protein fare. In the 1980s and 1990s it consisted of high complex carbohydrate fare. Now with the resurrection of the Atkins diet (aka "ketogenics"), high protein fare is making a comeback. Clearly, both of these treatments can't be correct.

In order to be a true hypoglycemic, you *must* possess a nonalkaline metabolic imbalance. So, the correct way to successfully treat this disorder is with high-purine fare. Note that I did *not* say "high-protein" fare, but rather "high-purine" fare. As stated in Chapter One, eggs, milk, cheese, chicken and turkey breast, and light meat fish are all high-protein foods whose purine composition is too low to correct an acid episode (and thus a hypoglycemic episode). Ending an acid episode with protein-rich foods that are purine-deficient is like trying to stop a freight train with a tissue paper barricade. To make matters worse, a high complex carbohydrate diet (typically prescribed for hypoglycemics) will worsen or accentuate the underlying acid imbalance, and thus aggravate a hypoglycemic condition. The well-intentioned health care provider who prescribes a high carbohydrate diet for a true hypoglycemic patient will send that patient spiraling downward into a hole of depression and disease.

This may seem a bit confusing to those of you who think that low blood sugar requires an additional intake of sugar (or carbohydrates, since sugar is a simple carbohydrate) to correct that dysfunction. But, If you are familiar with the laws of metabolic rate kinetics—unlike most health care providers—you know that increased carbohydrate intake will *further* accelerate the rate at which you oxidize or burn up blood sugar. This statement is true irrespective of how "complex" those carbohydrates may be. However, acceleration in blood glucose oxidation is precisely what you want to *avoid* if you are a nonalkaline metabolizer (true hypoglycemic) because you are already burning up or oxidizing glucose or blood sugar too rapidly.

Conversely, an acceleration of this nature is precisely what you want to achieve if you are an alkaline metabolizer (and therefore *not* hypoglycemic) because you are oxidizing glucose too slowly. The health care community has come up with some nonsensical, pseudo-scientific rationales for its dietary therapies in its war against hypoglycemia. At best these strategies have been only partially successful. Many of them have backfired and caused substantial patient harm. Of course, when all treatments fail, the patient is blamed, and shuffled off to the ever-ready sensitive expert for intensive psychotherapy.

The medical community's attempt to non-invasively treat diabetes is just as illogical as is its attempt to treat hypoglycemia. By way of brief summary, diabetes reflects a partial or complete failure of the pancreas to secrete insulin, a hormone needed to prevent blood glucose or sugar levels from rising to dangerously high levels. Consequently, the last thing a diabetic needs is a diet that will further raise his/her blood sugar levels and thereby further tax his/her pancreas into producing more insulin. By now you know that the most effective way of nutritionally raising your blood glucose levels is by ingesting purine-rich foods. Tragically, the history of the medical community's dietary treatment plans for diabetes track its treatment plans for hypoglycemia. In fact, I've worked with more than a few hypoglycemics who've been told that their condition was some sort of precursor to diabetes. Nothing could be further from the truth.

First of all diabetes reflects a pancreatic failure which limits insulin production resulting in excessively high levels of blood glucose. Hypoglycemia on the other hand is a systemic failure of intermediary metabolism, in which blood sugar is metabolized too rapidly, which results in chronic downshifting in venous plasma pH (an acid imbalance), which in turn is synonymous with low blood sugar levels. You can see that diabetes and hypoglycemia describe conditions at extreme opposite ends of the spectrum. Only ignorance could somehow connect them.

Nevertheless, medical attempts to nutritionally control diabetes have also swung from high protein fare to high carbohydrate fare. You should realize by now that effective nutritional treatment of diabetes consists of a low-purine, high complex carbohydrate regimen, namely the regimen appropriate for alkaline metabolizers. Why? Because by reducing blood sugar levels via biocompatible nutritional intervention, i.e. through a high complex carbohydrate, purine-deficient regime, there is less of a demand made on the pancreas to secrete insulin. More than a few diabetics who have achieved BioBalance have found that they could either reduce or in some cases eliminate their need for medication by adhering to the regimen appropriate for alkaline metabolizers.

Two important developments further substantiate the need to add BioBalance thinking to the diagnosis and treatment of blood sugar-related disorders:

- Relatively high doses of insulin ("insulin shock therapy") were historically administered to emotionally distressed individuals in treating chronic depression as well as other so-called mental disorders with significant success. The trouble with insulin shock therapy was that while many patients showed marked improvement, others got worse. Given what you know about metabolic diversity, and given the fact that individuals possess BioProfiles while disorders do not, you should now be able to understand precisely why the outcome of insulin therapy has been so varied. In any event, while insulin therapy's outcome is not always predictable and sometimes includes unexpected side effects, BioBalance Therapy's outcome is predictable, and unwanted side effects are nonexistent.

• Similarly, at the other end of the acid/alkaline metabolic spectrum, the medical profession recently made the following observation: while light fare (low fat/low cholesterol/high complex carbohydrate cuisine) was effective in reducing serum cholesterol and low-density lipids and triglycerides, more than a few individuals who ate in this fashion developed significant chronic emotional distress. The medical profession found this observation puzzling and mystifying. Once again, given what you've learned about BioBalance and metabolic diversity, I trust that you now understand precisely why this unfortunate situation took place. Furthermore, you should also understand why psychotherapy is really no solution at all in alleviating this resultant emotional distress.

In closing, to paraphrase the prologue to this book, it's up to you, dear reader, to implement BioBalance Therapy, since it has become painfully and abundantly clear that the established experts will probably continue to turn a blind eye and deaf ear to BioBalance Therapy. There is too much at stake for them. I have done my very best to make the application and understanding of BioBalance as simple as possible. Specifically, I have tried to keep the promise I made to you in Chapter One. I have made the application of BioBalance Therapy both as *fool-proof* and *fail-proof* as possible. In that regard and in conclusion, I trust the information I have provided in this book will allow you to embark upon a final and successful quest to achieve physical and psychological well-being.

Appendix

NOTE: The nutritional guidelines listed below offer maximum variety. While they overlap with the premier regimens listed in Chapter Two, the guidelines in this appendix are slightly different from the premier regimens listed in Chapter Two. Chapter Two shows you how and why it may be advisable for you to eat lower off the food chain irrespective of your metabolic type. Specifically, the information in Chapter Two makes it possible for you to do the following:

- If you are an alkaline metabolizer, you may achieve BioBalance while simultaneously abstaining from dairy, eggs, pork and poultry/fowl (a subset of the nutritional regimen outlined below). If you are an alkaline metabolizer, you may even find it possible to become a vegetarian *if and only if* you pursue the guidelines discussed in Chapter Two. Specifically, if you are an alkaline metabolizer and you abstain from all low purine protein derived from animal sources, then you *must* eat a small/modest amount of legumes - despite the fact that alkaline metabolizers are cautioned to avoid these foods under other circumstances - for both lunch and dinner in order to receive all of the essential amino acids (see Chapters One and Two).

- If you are a nonalkaline metabolizer, you may achieve BioBalance while simultaneously abstaining from dairy, eggs, pork, poultry/fowl as well as red meat (a subset of the nutritional regimen outlined below). If you are a nonalkaline metabolizer, and if you follow the guidelines discussed in Chapter Two, you *must* rely upon purine-rich seafood as part of your core regimen (see Chapters One and Two).

Consequently, *if you are a nonalkaline metabolizer, becoming a vegetarian is not advisable under any set of circumstances.*

Nevertheless, you are urged to read this appendix as well as Chapters One and Two thoroughly to familiarize yourself with the core regimen compatible with each metabolic type as well as with each premier regimen. You should attempt to implement the variations discussed in Chapter Two (the premier regimens) *when and only when* you have satisfactorily determined your metabolic type, and *when and only when* you have achieved BioBalance with your biocompatible nutrition regimen(s) outlined below.

A final note about caloric intake. Although I discuss calories in my first book, subsequent experience has taught me that counting calories is simply a waste of time. Individuals are encouraged to eat slowly, chew their foods thoroughly, and stop eating when they are satisfied.

– I –
Nutritional Regimen Appropriate for Alkaline Metabolizers
(The Alkaline-Compatible Regimen)

MEAT, FISH, POULTRY

ALLOWED: All light fish (preferrably fresh) such as scrod, cod, flounder, sole, turbot, perch, haddock and fancy solid white albacore tuna (packed in water), chicken and turkey breast, including low salt/low fat cold cuts and chicken/turkey franks/hot-dogs if and only if they are made from white meat chicken and turkey.

AVOID: Organ meats such as liver, kidneys, brains, sweet breads, tongue, tripe, bone marrow ("osso bucco"), etc.; pork ribs, bacon, all red meats including venison and veal, lamb, cold cuts of any variety (except those listed above), dark meat poultry (either chicken or turkey) such as poultry wings, thighs and drumsticks, duck and goose, all darker meat fish such as salmon (red and pink) and dark meat tuna, mackerel, sardines, anchovies, herrings, fish roe/caviar, mussels, scallops, clams, oysters, abalone, lobster, crab, shrimp, crayfish, snails, squid, octopus, all frankfurters of any variety, including chicken and turkey franks (except those listed above), beef franks, pork franks, soy/tofu franks, pork and ham.

Meat, fish and poultry of the allowed varieties should *never* be eaten at breakfast, and may be often skipped at lunch as well. They should be part of the dinner meal.

VEGETABLES

ALLOWED: Lettuce, tomatoes, cucumbers, peppers, garlic, horseradish, onions, leeks, scallions, cabbage, broccoli, broccoli raabe, collards, mustard greens, kale, carrots, parsnips, rutabagas, turnips, daikon radish, red radish, burdock root, lotus root, eggplant, brussel sprouts, bean sprouts, zucchini, summer sqaush, autumnal or pumpkin-like squash, spaghetti squash, kale, beets, potatoes, and sweet potatoes.

AVOID: All leguminous vegetables such as peas, beans, lentils of any variety including tofu (soy bean curd), fried or buttered potatoes (fats will be discussed below), spinach, cauliflower, artichokes and artichoke hearts, asparagus.

FUNGI

AVOID: All mushrooms.

FRUITS

ALLOWED: Apples and pears. All melons and citrus fruit such as oranges, tangerines, grapefruits, lemons, limes, pineapples, tangerines, tangeloes, plums, apricots, peaches, berries, cherries and grapes.

AVOID: Avocadoes, olives and bananas.

DAIRY

ALLOWED: Any dairy whose fat content is less than or equal to 1% (hereafter referred to as low fat dairy). If a lactose intolerance exists, all dairy should be lactose reduced, or if unavailable in this form, should be pretreated with Lactaid. This intolerance may subside after BioBalance is achieved.

AVOID: Any dairy or cheese whether it is made from cow's milk or goat's milk if its fat content equals or exceeds 2%; half and half, heavy cream, etc.

All low fat dairy may be used as a substitute for meat, fish and poultry for breakfast, and for lunch as well. If a lactose intolerance persists, then dairy should be avoided completely.

EGGS

ALLOWED: Eggs should not be a regular part of an alkaline metabolizer's regimen. An occasional egg (either hard boiled, poached or fried in Teflon and not butter), and preferably later in the day, is acceptable.

WHOLE GRAINS

ALLOWED: Most whole grains including brown rice, millet, buckwheat, whole barley, oats, rye, wheat, corn and amaranth. Essene (pronounced. "ah-seen") bread, Ezekial bread and rice cakes are primary choices among breads in that they contain no processed grain. It should be noted that all breads (whether processed or unprocessed) are to be used sparingly. Whole grains should be eaten daily as a side dish for at least two meals to assist in maintaining normal bowel function.

AVOID: None.

NUTS AND NUT BUTTERS

AVOID: All nuts, peanuts and seeds as well as nut and seed butters.

FATS

ALLOWED: Sesame seed oil in small quantities may be used for occasional stir frying. Olive oil (preferably extra-virgin, cold pressed), safflower, canola or corn oil, soy or safflower margarine, mayonnaise. *All fats should be used sparingly* despite the fact that they are listed as allowed.

AVOID: Butter and lard.

BEVERAGES

ALLOWED: Fruit juices, preferably *not* from concentrate. Soft drinks and alcoholic beverages may be used very sparingly and ideally avoided. Coffee (nondecaffeinated) and tea (nondecaffeinated) may be used in moderation. As BioBalance is achieved, caffeine tolerance will generally decrease (see Chapter Three).

AVOID: Technically, decaffeinated beverages need not be avoided. Nevertheless, it should be noted that they have no therapeutic value in off-setting an underlying alkaline metabolic imbalance.

MISCELLANEOUS

ALLOWED: Lean dilute, clarified chicken broth; dehydrated bullion cubes (try to avoid monosodium glutamate), mustard (preferably low salt), low salt ketchup, low salt horse radish, low salt hot sauce, low salt/low fat mayonnaise may be used sparingly, low salt/low fat salad dressing (preferrably free of additives and/or preservatives), fresh or powdered garlic, vinegar, low salt/low fat tomato based soups and sauces; dilute shoyu, miso and tamari or soy sauces (again, preferrably additive-free and preservative-free).

AVOID: Excess salt, meat and poultry gravies of any variety, rich poultry and beef stock; creamy based sauces and soups made with whole milk, half and half or heavy cream (such as New England clam/fish chowder).

DESSERTS

ALLOWED: Subject to the warning that all deserts should be used very sparingly, the following deserts are allowed: zero or low fat sherbet, low fat crust fruit pies.
AVOID: Ice cream, cheese cake, butter based pastries.

A NOTE ON RESTAURANT DINING

Many restaurants offer an acceptable fresh "Catch of the Day". Broiled or baked fish without fatty/buttery sauces and gravies are acceptable. Fried seafood should be avoided. If appropriate seafood is not available then chicken or turkey breast may be ordered. All fast foods should be avoided. Ideally, salt should not be added. Foods should be kept as additive-free and preservative-free as possible.

METHODS OF PREPARATION

Any method of preparation is acceptable except frying which is why fast foods are to be avoided. Stir frying is permitted if *small* amounts of allowed fats are used to coat the wok or skillet to prevent sticking.

TYPICAL BREAKFAST LUNCH AND DINNER FOR
ALKALINE METABOLIZERS

BREAKFAST: 1 cup of regular coffee, 1 glass of orange juice, 1 bowl of shredded wheat with lactose reduced low fat milk.

MID MORNING SNACK (optional): 1 cup of regular coffee or weakly brewed tea and fruit.

LUNCH: Salad consisting of pasta, lettuce, tomatoes, radishes, onions, peppers, cucumbers (peeled if waxed), shredded cabbage, broccoli; a low fat yogurt dressing is permitted if desired, or a small amount of olive oil and vinegar or lemon juice is permitted.

MID AFTERNOON SNACK (optional): 1 cup of regular coffee or tea plus 1 peeled, cored apple or 1 tangerine.

DINNER: Fillet of sole baked with lemon and a teaspoon of safflower oil; steamed zucchini and tomatoes, baked potato and brown rice; 1 cup of herbal tea.

The alkaline-appropriate nutritional regimen is not a "high coffee" diet. Most alkaline metabolizers rely upon coffee medicinally at first averaging 2 to 3 cups per day during the first several weeks of BioBalance Therapy. Later they may require 1 cup per day or none at all.

SUPPLEMENTS APPROPRIATE for ALKALINE METABOLIZERS
(THE ALKALINE-COMPATIBLE SUPPLEMENTS)

Supplements should never be taken until after a period of 30 days. In the event these supplements cannot be tolerated, they should not be taken.

It is suggested that all vitamins be taken in hypoallergenic form. A variation of 25% in the dosages given below should not affect therapeutic outcome.

A full dose (as listed below) should be taken after breakfast and again after lunch.

Vitamin/Mineral	Full Dose
A (fish liver oil)	10,000 IUs
D	400 IUs
C (any variety)	500 mgs
B1	10 mgs
B2	10 mgs
B6	10 mgs
Niacin	25 mgs
Para Amino Benzoic Acid	100 mgs
Folic Acid	200 mcgs
Biotin	150 mcgs
Potassium	100 mgs
Magnesium	100 mgs
Iron	15 mgs
Copper	1 mg
Manganese	5 mgs
Chromium	100 mcgs

All minerals should ideally be chelated. As far as dosages are concerned, the "elemental" quantity specified on the bottle's label and not the chelated amount constitute the full dose. For example, assume the label lists each tablet as containing 300 mgs of potassium chelate which in turn contains 99 mgs of elemental potassium. In this case then, 1 tablet would satisfy the full dose requirement listed above.

– II –
Nutritional Regimen Appropriate for Acid Metabolizers
(The Acid-Compatible Regimen)

MEAT, FISH, POULTRY

ALLOWED: Organ meats such as liver, kidneys, brains, sweet breads, tongue, tripe, bonme marrow, etc.; pork ribs, bacon, all red meats including venison and veal, lamb, cold cuts of any variety but preferably additive-free, dark meat poultry (either chicken or turkey) such as poultry wings, thighs and drumsticks (skin may be left on when fried as desired (see methods of preparation below), duck and goose, all darker meat fish such as salmon and dark meat tuna (either fresh, frozen or canned and packed in oil), mackerel, sardines, herrings, fish roe, caviar, mussels, scallops, clams, oysters, abalone, lobster, crab, shrimp, crayfish, snails, squid, octopus, frankfurters preferably additive-free, including chicken franks, beef franks, pork franks, soy/tofu franks, ham and pork; (ham and pork are "transition foods," which shouldn't really form the core regimen for acid metabolizers).

AVOID: All light fish (either fresh or frozen) such as scrod, cod, flounder, sole, turbot, perch, haddock and fancy solid white albacore tuna, chicken and turkey breast, lean pork, ham.

Meat, fish and poultry of the allowed varieties should be eaten at every meal. Abstention from allowed meat, fish and poultry will accentuate the underlying acid imbalance.

VEGETABLES

ALLOWED: All leguminous vegetables such as peas, beans, lentils of any variety including tofu (soy bean curd), fried or buttered potatoes (fats will be discussed below), carrots, celery, spinach, cauliflower, artichokes and artichoke hearts, asparagus, buttered squash (any variety except zucchini, summer squash and spaghetti squash). Some root vegetables may be used in moderation such as burdock root, daikon, lotus root, rutabagas, parsnips, turnips, etc.

AVOID: Lettuce, tomatoes, cucumbers, peppers, garlic, horseradish, onions, leeks, scallions, cabbage, broccoli, broccoli raabe, mustard greens, eggplant, brussel sprouts, bean sprouts, zucchini, spaghetti squash, kale, beets, sweet potatoes and yams.

FUNGI

ALLOWED: All mushrooms.

FRUITS

ALLOWED: Avocadoes and olives. Bananas may be used sparingly as desert or part of a meal. No more than 2 or 3 bananas should be consumed weekly. Apples and pears may be eaten cored and peeled, sparingly if desired and preferably with a generous amount of nut or seed butter and/or at the end of an appropriate meal (as dessert).

AVOID: All melons and citrus fruit (whether fresh or from concentrate) such as oranges, tangerines, grapefruits, lemons, limes, pineapples, tangerines and tangeloes. The following fruits may be used very sparingly: apples, pears, plums, apricots, peaches, berries, cherries and grapes.

DAIRY

All dairy and eggs (below) should be used sparingly, and not as protein substitute for allowed meats, fish and poultry.

ALLOWED: Any whole dairy or cheese whether it made from cow's milk or goat's milk; half and half, heavy cream. If a lactose intolerance exists, all dairy should be lactose reduced or if unavailable in this form, should be pretreated with Lactaid. This intolerance may subside after BioBalance is achieved.

AVOID: Any dairy whose fat content is less than or equal to 2%.

EGGS

ALLOWED: Eggs may be prepared in any fashion. As is the case with whole dairy, eggs should not be regarded as a primary source of protein and as such should not be viewed as a substitute for appropriate meats, fish or poultry. To re-emphasize a point made earlier, as far as acid metabolizers are concerned, any meal lacking the allowed meats, fish and/or poultry is simply not a meal.

WHOLE GRAINS

ALLOWED: All whole grains. Whole grains include brown rice, millet, buckwheat, whole barley, corn, oats, rye, wheat and amaranth. Essene bread or Ezekial bread and rice cakes are primary choices among breads in that they contain no processed grain. Essene or Ezekial breads or rice cakes with generous amounts of nut or seed butters make excellent snacks. It should be noted that all breads (whether processed or unprocessed) are to be used sparingly. Whole grains should be eaten daily as a side dish for at least 2 meals to assist in detoxification and subsequent normal bowel function.

AVOID: Any processed breakfast cereal (whether sugar free or containing sugar), either hot or cold.

NUTS AND NUT BUTTERS

ALLOWED: All nuts, peanuts and seeds as well as nut and seed butters.

AVOID: None.

FATS

ALLOWED: Toasted sesame oil for stir frying; corn, safflower oil may also be used in stir frying, but toasted sesame oil is preferred; olive oil and butter

AVOID: None.

BEVERAGES

ALLOWED: Decaffeinated coffee and tea. Weak dilute tea. Weak dilute fruit juice (preferably not citrus or juice derived from concentrate) may be used sparingly and as part of a meal. For example, dilute (1/2 apple juice + 1/2 water is allowed) and preferably with a meal.

AVOID: Soft drinks and alcoholic beverages. Coffee, tea and all undiluted fruit juices.

MISCELLANEOUS

ALLOWED: Salt to taste, fresh (home made) meat and poultry gravies of any variety, rich fresh made poultry or beef stock (not all the fat should be skimmed); a cup of meat and poultry stock prepared in this fashion makes an excellent snack. Creamy based sauces and soups made with whole milk, half and half or heavy cream (such as New England clam or fish chowder made with generous amounts of allowed meats and fish). Concentrated shoyu, miso, tamari and soy sauce are permitted.

AVOID: Lean dilute, clarified chicken broth may be used sparingly but not as a primary source of sustenance; dehydrated bullion cubes, monosodium glutamate, mustard, ketchup, horse radish, hot sauce, mayonnaise, salad dressing, fresh or powdered garlic, vinegar. Tomato based soups and sauces.

DESSERTS

ALLOWED: Subject to the warning that all deserts should be used *very sparingly,* the following deserts are allowed: ice cream, cheese cake, butter based pastries (provided that they contain little if any jam or jelly).

AVOID: Zero or low fat sherbet, fruit pies and fruit torts.

A NOTE ON RESTAURANT DINING

While fast food dining is not encouraged, eating purine-rich fast food in event of an emergency is acceptable and is far superior to eating nothing at all. Fasting is ill-advised for acid metabolizers. In any event, planning ahead is a rule which should be observed. Standard fast food fare such as hamburgers, cheeseburgers, bacon burgers, etc. (without excessive condiments) is acceptable in an emergency. White meat chicken, pasta salads, etc., are ill-advised for acid metabolizers.

METHODS OF PREPARATION

Any method of preparation is acceptable. Sauteeing and stir frying are encouraged.

TYPICAL BREAKFAST, LUNCH and DINNER for ACID TYPES

BREAKFAST: Sausage links (not spicy) with hash browns fried in a small amount of butter or residual sausage fat; 1 cup of decaffeinated coffee with half and half.

MID MORNING SNACK (optional): 1 thin slice of Essene bread with any choice of nut or seed butter.

LUNCH: Salmon salad with generous amounts of salmon, plus spinach, garbanzo beans, artichoke hearts, mushrooms and asparagus tips; dressing to consist of 1/4 wedge of fresh squeezed lemon, olive oil, salt to taste; 1 cup of decaffeinated herbal tea.

MID AFTERNOON SNACK (optional): 1 cup of fresh made meat or poultry stock, and/or 1/4 apple with any choice of nut or seed butter.

DINNER: Cup of split pea soup, chicken liver (with small amount of sauteed onion) sauteed in butter, stir fried carrots, cauliflower and brown rice, 1 cup of herbal tea.

It cannot be emphasized too strongly that as far as this regimen is concerned (appropriate for acid types only), any meal lacking meat, fish or poultry of the allowed variety is not appropriate.

SUPPLEMENTS APPROPRIATE for ACID METABOLIZERS (ACID-COMPATIBLE SUPPLEMENTS)

Supplements should never be taken until after a period of 30 days. In the event these supplements cannot be tolerated, they should not be taken.

It is suggested that all vitamins be taken in hypoallergenic form. A variation of 25% in the dosages given below should not affect therapeutic outcome.

A full dose (as listed below) should be taken after breakfast and again after lunch.

Vitamin/Mineral	Full Dose
A (palmitate)	10,000 IUs
E (mixed tocopherols)	400 IUs
B12	100 mcgs
C (any variety)	250 mgs
Niacinamide	100 mgs
Pantothenic Acid	100 mgs
Inositol	250 mgs
Choline	250 mgs
Calcium	500 mgs
Phosphorous	250 mgs
Iodine (derived from kelp)	0.15 mgs
Zinc	10 mgs

All minerals should ideally be chelated. Iodine will likely not be found in chelated form. Kelp is commonly the supplemental form for iodine. As far as dosages are concerned, the "elemental" quantity specified on the bottle's label and not the chelated amount constitute the full dose. For example, assume the label lists each tablet as containing 100 mgs of zinc chelate which in turn contains 10 mgs of elemental zinc. In this case then, 1 tablet would satisfy the full dose requirement listed above.

— III —
Nutritional Regimen Appropriate for Mixed Mode Metabolizers
(The Mixed-Compatible Regimen)

This nutritional regimen consists of a combination of the regimen appropriate for acid and alkaline metabolizers. This regimen is biased more heavily in favor of the regimen appropriate for acid metabolizers because mixed metabolizers resemble acid metabolizers far more so than they resemble alkaline metabolizers. Accordingly, the food categories given here are listed as "primary" and "secondary". The ratio of primaries to secondaries may vary from 2:1 to 4:1 without altering the therapeutic outcome of this regimen. Examples will be given below to explain more fully how this regimen should be administered.

MEAT, FISH, POULTRY

PRIMARY: Organ meats such as liver, kidneys, brains, sweet breads, tongue, tripe, bone marrow, etc.; pork ribs, bacon, all red meats including venison and veal, lamb, cold cuts of any variety but preferably additive-free, dark meat poultry (either chicken or turkey) such as poultry wings, thighs and drumsticks (skin may be left on or removed when fried as desired — see methods of preparation below), duck and goose, all darker meat fish such as salmon and dark meat tuna (either fresh, frozen or canned and packed in oil), mackerel, sardines, herrings, fish roe, caviar, mussels, scallops, clams, oysters, abalone, lobster, crab, shrimp, crayfish, snails, squid, octopus, all frankfurters of any variety but preferably additive-free, including chicken franks, beef franks, pork franks, soy/tofu franks.

SECONDARY: All light fish (either fresh or frozen) such as scrod, cod, flounder, sole, turbot, perch, haddock and fancy solid white albacore tuna, chicken and turkey breast, lean pork, ham.

Meat, fish and poultry of both the primary and secondary varieties should be eaten at lunch and dinner. This meat, fish and poultry may either be eaten or avoided at breakfast depending upon the response of the mixed mode metabolizer. This determination is typically determined via trial and error. In this regard, mixed metabolizers fall into two subclasses, those who can tolerate lighter fare for breakfast, and those who cannot. In any event, these two subclasses typically face similar if not identical nutritional requirements for both lunch and dinner.

VEGETABLES

PRIMARY: All leguminous vegetables such as peas, beans, lentils of any variety including tofu (soy bean curd), fried or buttered potatoes (fats will be discussed below), carrots, celery, spinach, cauliflower, artichokes and artichoke hearts, asparagus, buttered squash.

SECONDARY: Lettuce, tomatoes, cucumbers, peppers, garlic, horseradish, onions, leeks, scallions, cabbage, broccoli, broccoli raabe, mustard greens, eggplant, brussel sprouts, bean sprouts, zucchini, spaghetti squash, kale, beets, sweet potatoes, yams, burdock root, daikon, lotus root, rutabagas, parsnips, turnips, etc..

FUNGI

PRIMARY: All mushrooms.

FRUITS

PRIMARY: Avocadoes and olives. Bananas may be used sparingly as desert or part of a meal. No more than 2 or 3 bananas should be consumed weekly. Apples and pears may be eaten cored and peeled, sparingly if desired and preferably with a generous amount of nut or seed butter at the end of an appropriate meal and/or as a snack.

SECONDARY: All melons and citrus fruit (whether fresh or from concentrate) such as oranges, tangerines, grapefruits, lemons, limes, pineapples, tangerines and tangeloes, plums, apricots, peaches, berries, cherries and grapes.

DAIRY

All dairy (and eggs) should be used sparingly, and not as a protein substitute for primary meats, fish and poultry.

PRIMARY: Any whole dairy or cheese whether it is made from cow's milk or goat's milk; half and half, heavy cream. If a lactose intolerance exists, all dairy should be lactose reduced or if unavailable in this form, should be pretreated with Lactaid. This intolerance may subside after BioBalance is achieved.

SECONDARY: Any dairy whose fat content is less than or equal to 2%.

EGGS

PRIMARY: Eggs may be prepared in any fashion. As is the case with whole dairy, eggs should not be regarded as a primary source of protein and as such should not be viewed as a substitute for appropriate meats, fish or poultry.

WHOLE GRAINS

PRIMARY: All whole grains. Whole grains include brown rice, millet, buckwheat, whole barley, corn, oats, rye, wheat and amaranth. Essene bread, Ezekial bread, and rice cakes are primary choices among breads in that they contain no processed grain (such as flour). Essene breads, Ezekial breads or rice cakes with nut or seed butters make excellent snacks. It should be noted that all breads (whether processed or unprocessed) are to be used sparingly. Whole grains should be eaten daily as a side dish for at least two meals per day to assist in maintaining normal bowel function and subsequent detoxification.

SECONDARY: Any processed breakfast cereal (whether sugar free or with sugar), either hot or cold. Once again, some mixed metabolizers find that a lighter breakfast is more tolerable than a heavier breakfast. Other mixed metabolziers cannot tolerate lighter fare for breakfast. This determination must be made via trial and error.

NUTS AND NUT BUTTERS

PRIMARY: All nuts, peanuts and seeds as well as nut and seed butters.

FATS

PRIMARY: Toasted sesame seed oil is preferrable when stir frying; olive oil (preferrably extra virgin and cold pressed) and butter; corn, safflower or canola oil may also be used in stir frying, but sesame oil is preferrable.

SECONDARY: Safflower, corn or canola oil (as a major source of fat), soy or safflower margarine, mayonnaise.

BEVERAGES

PRIMARY: Decaffeinated coffee and tea. Weak dilute tea. Weak dilute fruit juice (preferably not citrus). For example, dilute (1/2 apple juice + 1/2 water is allowed) and preferably with a meal.

SECONDARY: Soft drinks and alcoholic beverages may be used very sparingly. Coffee, tea and all undiluted fruit juices may be used very sparingly or avoided.

MISCELLANEOUS

PRIMARY: Salt to taste, fresh (home made) meat and poultry gravies of any variety, rich fresh-made poultry or beef stock (not all the fat should be skimmed); meat and poultry stock prepared in this fashion makes an excellent snack. Creamy based sauces and soups made with whole milk, half and half or heavy cream (such as New England clam chowder). Soyu, miso, tamari and soy sauce are permitted.

SECONDARY: Lean dilute, clarified chicken broth may be used sparingly but not as a primary source of sustenance; dehydrated bullion cubes, mustard, ketchup, horse radish, hot sauce, mayonnaise, salad dressing, fresh or powdered garlic, vinegar. Tomato based soups and sauces.

DESSERTS

PRIMARY: Subject to the warning that all desserts should be used very sparingly, the following deserts are allowed: ice cream, cheese cake, butter based pastries.

SECONDARY: Zero or low fat sherbet such as sorbet, fruit pies and fruit torts.

A NOTE ON RESTAURANT DINING

While fast food dining is not encouraged, eating high protein (i.e., meat) fast food fare in event of an emergency is acceptable and is far advantageous to eating nothing at all. In any event, planning ahead is a rule which should be observed. Standard fast food fare such as a hamburger, cheeseburger or bacon burger is acceptable in an emergency.

METHODS OF PREPARATION

Any method of preparation is acceptable. Sauteeing and stir frying are encouraged.

TYPICAL BREAKFAST LUNCH AND DINNER FOR MIXED METABOLIZERS

Some mixed metabolizers require primary meats, fish and/or poultry for breakfast while others do not. This is a judgment call that must be made by each mixed metabolizer through trial-and-error. Some mixed metabolizers may even eat light breakfasts (resembling breakfasts appropriate for alkaline types), but they *must* eat primary meats, seafood and/or poultry for lunch *and* dinner. Individuals within this mixed metabolic subgroup have even found that they may abstain from breakfast on occasion and feel well until mid-day. They find, however, that their cognitive/mental function becomes substantially impaired if they continue to fast or eat light during mid-day and beyond. It would be an error to classify this subgroup of mixed metabolizers as diurnal cyclers for the following 3 reasons:

- Diurnal cyclers are extremely rare (less than 1%), whereas nearly half of all mixed metabolizers (half of 12.5% of the population in general) plus all alkaline metabolizers find that they do best if they "eat light" or very little for breakfast.
- Diurnal cyclers generally tend to cycle through all three static metabolic states through the course of 24 hours.
- Virtually *all* mixed metabolizers who can tolerate supplements find that they can tolerate *only* mixed-compatible supplements throughout the course of the day. In this context, members of the mixed subgroup who do best by eating light breakfasts *cannot* tolerate alkaline-compatible supplements for breakfast, thus disqualifying them from being classified as diurnal cyclers.

As I stated previously, most individuals' BioProfiles are static and relatively uncomplicated. Cyclic BioProfiles generally cycle over 28 days, and transition between two static metabolic states. Consequently, unless your caffeine tolerance response suggests otherwise, your BioProfile is probably not ornate.

OPTION A - "HEAVIER" REGIMEN FOR MIXED METABOLIZERS

BREAKFAST: Sausage links with hash browned potatoes fried in a small amount of butter or residual sausage fat; 1 glass of apple juice; 1 cup of weak coffee or decaf coffee with whole milk.

MID MORNING SNACK (optional): 1/2 an apple with any choice of nut or seed butter, herbal tea.

LUNCH: Salad with generous amounts of dark tuna (chunk light) and some fancy white albacore tuna, small amounts of cherry tomatoes, shredded cucumbers, and generous portions of spinach, garbanzo beans, artichoke hearts, asparagus tips; dressing to consist of 1/2 wedge of fresh squeezed lemon, olive oil, salt to taste; 2 rice cakes; 1 cup of herbal tea.

MID AFTERNOON SNACK (optional): 1 cup of fresh made meat or poultry stock, and/or 1/2 apple with any choice of nut or seed butter.

DINNER: Cup of split pea soup (preferrably home made), chicken liver (with medium amount of sauteed onion) sauteed in butter, stir fried carrots and broccoli, brown rice, 1 cup of herbal tea.

OPTION B - "LIGHTER" REGIMEN FOR MIXED METABOLIZERS

BREAKFAST: unprocessed whole grain cereal with tofu, or oatmeal with lactose reduced milk ranging from 1% milk fat to whole milk, or yogurt (1% to whole) with small amount of nuts, seeds and mixed fruit; 1 glass of whole fresh juice (any fresh fruit juice not from concentrate); 1 cup of weak coffee or decaf coffee with milk (1% to whole) or herbal/decaf tea.

MID MORNING SNACK (optional): 1/2 an apple with any choice of nut butter, herbal tea.

LUNCH: Cup of New England clam chowder (preferably additive-free); chicken salad sandwich with light and dark meat chicken with mayonnaise and chopped onions and celery on Ezekial bread; 1 cup of herbal tea.

MID AFTERNOON SNACK (optional): 1 cup of fresh made meat or poultry stock, or 1/2 apple with any choice of nut or seed butter.

DINNER: Cup of bean soup (preferably additive-free), lightly batter-fried chicken thigh, mashed potatoes with pat of butter, sauteed broccoli and cauliflower, and brown rice, 1 cup of herbal tea.

Options A and B are heavier and lighter variants respectively of the regimen appropriate for mixed metabolizers. Once again, some mixed metabolizers do better on option A while others do better on option B. In either event it would be an error to eat either as an acid metabolizer or as an alkaline metabolizer, thinking perhaps that either extreme can be offset by the supplements appropriate for mixed metabolizers (given below). If a mixed metabolizer is to err, that error should be made in favor of eating foods more appropriate for an acid metabolizer for both lunch and dinner, and *perhaps* for breakfast as well. It has already been mentioned that a mixed metabolzier resembles an acid metabolizer more so than an alkaline metabolizer. Nevertheless it would also be a serious error if a mixed metabolizer avoided all of the "secondary" foods.

SUPPLEMENTS APPROPRIATE for MIXED METABOLIZERS (MIXED-COMPATIBLE SUPPLEMENTS)

Supplements should never be taken until after a period of 30 days. In the event these supplements cannot be tolerated, they should not be taken.

It is suggested that all vitamins be taken in hypoallergenic form. A variation of 25% in the dosages given below should not affect therapeutic outcome.

A full dose should be taken after breakfast and again after lunch.

Your health food store or pharmacy may (for a fee) grind and encapsulate these supplements for your convenience so that you will only have to take several capsules after each of breakfast and lunch rather than an assortment of pills and tablets. If you or your supplier is unwilling to do so, then you will have to purchase several different supplements and take them accordingly to satisfy the supplemental requirements listed below.

Vitamin/Mineral	Full Dose
A (palmitate)	5,000 IUs
A (fish liver oil)	5,000 IUs
D	400 IUs
C (any variety)	500 mgs
E (mixed tocopherols)	400 IUs
B1	10 mgs
B2	10 mgs
B6	10 mgs
B12	100 mcgs
Niacinamide	100 mgs
Pantothenic Acid	100 mgs
Para-Amino Benzoic Acid	100 mgs
Inositol	250 mgs
Choline	250 mgs
Calcium	500 mgs
Phosphorous	250 mgs
Iodine (derived from kelp)	0.15 mgs
Folic Acid	200 mcgs
Biotin	150 mcgs
Potassium	200 mgs
Magnesium	100 mgs
Iron	15 mgs
Copper	1 mg
Manganese	5 mgs
Chromium	100 mcgs
Zinc	10 mgs

All minerals should ideally be chelated. Iodine will likely not be found in chelated form. Kelp is commonly the supplemental form for iodine. Insofar as dosages are concerned, the "elemental" quantity specified on the bottle's label and not the chelated amount constitute the full dose. For example, assume the label lists each tablet as containing 100 mgs of zinc chelate which in turn contains 10 mgs of elemental zinc. In this case then, 1 tablet would satisfy the full dose requirement listed above.

A full dose may be taken after breakfast and again after lunch.

References

EXPERIMENTAL and CLINICAL OBSERVATIONS
1. Watson, G.; Comfrey, A.L.; J. Psych., (1954), 38, 251-264.
2. Watson, G.; J. Psych., (1957), 43, 47-63.
3. Watson, G.; Currier, W.D.; J. Psych.., (1960), 49, 67-81.
4. Watson, G.; Psych Rep., (1960), 6, 602.
5. Watson, G.; Psych. Rep., (1965), 17, 149-170.
6. Wiley, R. A.; Int. J. Biosocial Res., 1987; (2); 182-202.

THEORETICAL ANALYSES
Wiley, R.A.; Silvidi, A.A.; J. Bio. Phys., (1982), 10, 31-42.
Wiley, R. A.; J. of Ideas., (1990), 1, 47-54.]
Kushi, M., Standard Macrobiotic Diet, (1996), One Peaceful World Press
Kushi, M., The Book of Macrobiotics, (1986), Japan Publications, Inc.

THE EFFECTIVENESS of PSYCHOTHERAPY
11. Prioleau, L.; Murdock, M., Brody, N.; The Behavioral and Brain Sciences, (1983), 6, 275-310.

BIOBALANCE
12. Wiley, R. A.; BIOBALANCE: Using Acid/Alkaline Nutrition to Solve the Food- Mood-Health Puzzle, ISBN: 0943685052, c. 1988, Essential Science Publishing, Tel. 801-224-6228; fax 801-224-6229. Website/email: www.essentialscience.net

Note: BioBalance may be purchased at many bookstores, and at Amazon.com as well as at Essential Science Publishing's website.

Biography

Dr. Rudolf A. Wiley holds an M.A. in psychology and a doctorate in biophysics. He has spent almost 30 years researching the relationship between metabolism, health and behavior. As director of his consulting firm, BIOBALANCE SERVICES, Dr. Wiley consulted with the medical community, and lectured before the Society for the Study of Biochemical Intolerances and the North American Nutrition and Preventive Medicine Association

In addition to authoring the book, *BIOBALANCE: The Acid/Alkaline Solution to the Food-Mood-Health Puzzle,* Dr. Wiley's scientific publications appear in the Journal of Biological Physics, the Journal of Ideas, and the International Journal of Biosocial Research.

BIOBALANCE²: Achieving Optimum Health through Acid/Alkaline Nutrition, Dr. Wiley's second major publication, presents BioBalance therapy in simplified terms and practical steps for the general public

BioBalance2

Index

absorption: 8
acid/alkaline: vii-ix, 3, 6-7, 9, 11, 16, 19-20, 27, 29, 44, 64, 121, 140, 155, 159-160, 164, 191, 193
acid regimen: 173
adrenals: 2, 9
adverse reaction: 18, 40, 67, 91, 105, 127, 145
alkaline regimen: 33, 167
all-natural: 19, 67, 77, 82
alternative health care: ix, 7-8, 27, 30
amalgam: 2
amino acids: 15, 19, 40, 165
animal foods: 16, 23, 37, 45, 48, 57-58, 114
anxiety: 0, 8, 22, 89, 105, 140, 150
attention: viii, 8, 67, 154
autocompensatory Response: 12, 119
bacteria: 8
basal metabolism: 20
behavioral disorders: 1, 8, 11, 26
beverages: 16, 37, 45, 169, 176, 184
BioBalance Matrix: 25
biochemical: v, 1, 3, 5, 7, 9, 15, 19, 40, 67, 119, 193
biochemical imbalance: 9, 11
biology: viii
BioProfile: 1-6, 8, 11, 13-15, 20-24, 30-32, 47-52, 55-57, 65, 68-69, 87, 118, 140, 148-150, 157, 159, 186
biotin: 17, 172, 189
bloating: 64, 140, 150
blood: viii, 1, 3-6, 9, 14, 20, 23, 90, 114, 149-150, 160, 162-163

blood glucose: 162-163
caffeine: 20-22, 37, 42, 46, 49-53, 55-57, 63-64, 141, 148-149, 157, 161, 169, 186
calcium: 17, 57, 179, 189
candidiasis: 2, 9, 41, 43, 90, 149, 159-160
carbohydrates: 15, 26, 90, 114, 162
cardiovascular: 140
chemistry: 5, 19
chi: 34
cholesterol: ix, 164
choline: 17, 57, 179, 189
chromium: 17, 172, 189
chronic fatigue: 2, 8, 22, 58, 64, 150-151
citrus: 16, 37, 45, 168, 174, 176, 183-184
coffee: 21-22, 37, 39, 41-42, 49, 51-52, 54-56, 67-75, 77-80, 82, 84-87, 92, 102, 105-106, 115-116, 120-123, 125-126, 128-129, 131-132, 142, 146-147, 169, 171, 176-177, 184, 187
concentrate: 150, 169, 174, 176, 183, 187
condiments: 38, 177
constipation: 64, 116
copper: 17, 172, 189
cyclic: 0, 9, 11, 21-22, 24, 26, 39, 50-52, 139-141, 143, 145, 147-148, 186
dairy: 19, 37, 39-40, 45, 57, 137, 165, 168, 174-175, 183

degenerative disease: 26, 33
dentist: 56
depression: 8, 11, 22, 55, 59, 64, 140, 150, 162-163
diabetes: 22, 24, 57, 90, 114, 160, 162-163
diabetic: 57, 90, 163
diagnosis: 159, 163
diagnostic tool: 30
ddiarrhea: 64
diet: vi, ix, 2, 12, 17-19, 27-28, 31-33, 42-43, 46-49, 57-59, 65-66, 68, 84, 90-91, 94-95, 97, 99, 101-102, 105-106, 110, 115, 120-121, 132, 135-136, 141, 143, 161-163, 171, 191
dosages: 172, 179, 188, 190
Dr. Richard Atkins: 18
dynamic equilibrium: 34
eggs: 19, 37, 39-40, 45, 102, 111, 115-116, 122, 136-137, 147, 162, 165, 168, 174-175, 183
elimination: 8, 32
enzyme: 19
Epstein-Barr: 2, 9, 159-160
exercise: ix, 6
fast: iv, 26, 35, 56-58, 170, 177, 185-186
fast food: 56, 177, 185
fasting: 42, 56, 177
fatigue: 2, 8, 22, 55, 58, 64, 121, 140, 150-151
fats: 15, 38, 40, 42, 65, 114, 140, 168-170, 173, 176, 182, 184
female: 22, 26, 34, 39, 50
fibromyalgia: 2, 22
fish: 16-17, 19, 23, 39, 44, 46, 48, 54, 56, 58, 65, 82, 84, 86, 114, 118, 124, 135, 137, 162, 167-168, 170, 172-176, 178, 181-183, 186, 189
folic acid: 17, 172, 189
food allergies: 2, 9
food challenge test: 22, 51-55, 57, 92, 94

Food/Mood Diary: 61, 69, 71-72, 74-76, 78-79, 81-82, 92, 119, 122-124, 126, 128-129, 131-133
frequency: 21, 26
fruit: v, 37, 45, 70, 73, 78, 84, 86-87, 114, 135, 137, 142, 146, 168-171, 174, 176-177, 183-185, 187
fungus: 8
garlic: 84-87, 167, 170, 174, 176, 182, 185
gas: 38, 64, 140
genetic: 10
George Watson: viii
glucose oxidation: viii, 162
glucose tolerance test: 114, 161
grains: 16, 35-40, 45-46, 116, 169, 175, 183
headaches: 8, 89, 150
holistic: ix, 2, 5, 22-23, 27, 32, 55, 58, 90, 159-161
hormone: 162
hot weather: 84
hunger: 54, 84, 96-97
hyperactivity: ix
hypoglycemia: 2, 9, 22-24, 90, 114, 160-163
immune system: 2, 9, 30, 43
inability to concentrate: 150
inositol: 17, 57, 179, 189
insomnia: 8, 64, 140, 150
insulin: 162-164
insurance: i, ix-x, 156-157
iodine: 17, 179, 189-190
iron: 17, 38, 172, 189
irritable bowel: 8
Isaac Newton: 29
jittery: 21, 99
ketogenic diet: 18
lactose intolerance: 40, 65, 168, 174, 183
leaky gut: 8-9
legumes: 16, 36, 38-42, 45-46, 58, 66-67, 140, 165
light: 18-19, 23, 26, 29, 37, 46-47, 65-66, 68, 86, 94, 103, 105, 108,

115-116, 118, 125, 135-136, 140-141, 143, 145, 154-155, 162, 164, 167, 173, 181, 186-188
light diet: 19, 46, 66, 143
macrobiotics: 31, 33-36, 39-41, 43-45, 48, 65, 84-85, 191
magnesium: 17, 172, 189
male: 34, 39, 50
manganese: 17, 172, 189
marker: 3, 5
meat: 16, 19-20, 23, 37, 44, 47-48, 56, 65, 84, 86-87, 100, 103, 108, 112, 114-116, 124-125, 128, 130, 133, 135-137, 147, 162, 165, 167-168, 170, 173, 176-178, 181-182, 184-185, 187-188
medical profession: 157, 164
medical school: viii-ix
menstrual cycles: 21-22, 24, 50-51, 140, 148
mental disorders: vii-viii, 163
mercury: 2
meta-analysis: 153
metabolic: v, 3, 5, 8-13, 15, 17-30, 32, 40, 43-55, 57, 59-61, 64, 67-68, 81, 84, 90-91, 94, 107, 118-119, 128, 137, 139-141, 143, 148-150, 155-156, 159-162, 164-166, 169, 186
metabolic rate kinetics: 10, 20, 160, 162
migraine: 89, 93, 95-96
mind/body: vii-viii
minerals: 14-15, 17, 63, 81, 89, 105, 107, 128, 172, 179, 190
misdiagnosis: 91, 151
mixed regimen: 25
mood: viii, 24, 50, 61, 69-83, 92-93, 95-105, 107-113, 119-134, 140-148
multiphasic inventories: 7
nervous: 8, 21, 49, 68, 92-93, 95-104, 107, 150
nervous stomach: 8
neurotic: 24
niacin: 17, 59, 68, 81, 172

niacinamide: 17, 179, 189
nucleoproteins: 15-16, 18-19, 42, 65, 95
nutrition: viii-ix, 2-3, 5, 24-25, 27-28, 32, 43, 58, 64, 68-69, 155, 166, 191, 193
nutritional mismatch: 10
olive oil: 38, 45, 71, 77, 82, 85-87, 93, 96-97, 100, 103, 109, 113, 115-116, 135-136, 147, 169, 171, 176-177, 184, 187
oscillations: 34
overweight: 64, 89
pancreatitis: 2, 9
panic: 8, 90, 92-93, 103, 111, 140, 143, 147, 150
pantothenic acid: 17, 179, 189
Para Amino Benzoic Acid (PABA): 17
peak wellness 4, 11
personality: 118
pH: viii, 5-9, 20, 40, 44, 149-150, 152, 159-161, 163
phosphorus: 17, 179, 189
physical: iv-v, vii, ix, 1-2, 4, 6-7, 9-11, 13, 59-60, 64, 67, 118, 139, 155, 164
physical activity: iv
physical fitness: ix
physicians: vi, ix-x, 1-2, 7, 34, 39, 41, 91, 114
physics: vii-ix, 154, 193
placebo: 7, 12, 30, 44, 152-154, 158
placebo effect: 7, 12, 30, 152
PMS: 8, 31, 50, 58, 140, 143-144, 148, 150-151
poultry: 16, 19, 23, 47-48, 56, 65, 84, 86, 114, 116, 118, 135, 137, 165, 167-168, 170, 173-176, 178, 181-184, 186-188
premenstrual syndrome: ix, 8, 22, 58, 140
preparation methods: 38, 170, 173, 177, 181, 185
prioleau: 152-153, 191
processed foods: 26, 45

protein: 15, 19, 46-48, 54, 57, 66, 161, 163, 165, 174-175, 183, 185
psychogenic: 1, 8, 43, 139, 151
psychological: viii, 1, 4, 7-8, 11, 13, 24, 43, 59, 121, 139, 150-152, 164
psychotherapy: 5, 24, 28, 30, 59, 119, 150-159, 162, 164, 191
purines: 15-16, 18-19, 42, 44, 65, 95
rebound reaction: 119
reductionism: 151, 156
regimen: v-vi, 2-4, 11-18, 23, 25, 31-33, 35, 39-40, 42-44, 47-49, 53, 57, 59, 63-67, 69, 81, 84-85, 89-91, 94, 104-105, 107, 114, 116-118, 121, 127-128, 135, 137-141, 143, 145, 163, 165-168, 171, 173, 178, 181, 187-188
relationships: viii
religion: 33-34
restaurant: 170, 177, 185
sauce: 72-73, 84-87, 108, 170, 176, 185
seafood: 16, 19, 23, 38, 40, 44-48, 87, 116, 165, 170, 186
shellfish: 44
soft drink: 52
soil: 6, 8
soup: 38, 46, 77, 83, 96-97, 100, 102, 104, 112, 115, 134, 136, 144, 178, 187-188
stiffness: 69, 77
stress: ix, 1, 6, 27, 58, 60, 118, 127, 150
stress related: 118, 127
suggestion: viii, 7, 12, 30, 60, 152
supermarket: iv
supplements: iv, 4, 11, 14-15, 17-18, 47, 53, 57, 59, 63, 68-69, 81-82, 89, 91-92, 94, 105-107, 111-112, 117-119, 127-128, 141, 145-148, 172, 179, 186, 188-189

tests: 4-5, 7-8, 14, 20, 23, 149, 152, 161
tired: 69-74, 77, 79, 83, 96-99, 112, 121, 123-125, 131, 142, 144, 146-147
tolerance: 22, 49-53, 55-57, 63, 114, 141, 148-149, 157, 161, 169, 186
triglycerides: 164
underweight: 90
vegetables: 16, 36, 38-39, 44-47, 86, 135, 137, 167-168, 173-174, 182
vegetarian: 54, 67, 76-77, 165-166
venous plasma pH: viii, 5-9, 20, 40, 44, 160-161, 163
vitamin A: 17, 58
vitamin B1: 17
vitamin B12: 17
vitamin B2: 17
vitamin B6: 17
vitamin C: 17, 89
vitamin D: 17
vitamin E: 17, 58
vitamins: ix, 14-15, 17, 58-59, 63, 81, 89, 105, 107, 128, 132, 172, 179, 188
weight: 8, 57, 59, 64, 90, 140, 150
weight management: 8
wellness: iii-vi, 4, 10-11, 13, 20, 23, 25-26, 48, 50, 52, 57, 59
wine: 37
within normal limits: x, 1
yang: 34-35
yeast: 2, 9, 90, 149, 160
yin: 34-35
zinc: 17, 179, 189-190